I0421040

WAR DIARY FROM BRUSSELS

Just
Three
Weeks
to
Baghdad

Ivan Herceg

C-Copyright:2013-Ivan Herceg

All Right Reserved

ISBN 13:978-1514889336

ISBN 10:1514889331

I dedicate this diary to all the innocent victims of our time and to world peace...

CONTENTS

PROLOG

WAR DIARY FROM BRUSSELS

I would like to thank all the war correspondents, especially those who are no longer with us...

Proofreader: Jim Newall

Design: Ivan Herceg
The cover is based on artistic works (9/11) of the author

PROLOG

A Last Thought from the Author

(*Spring 2003*)

I hate any war, but I do understand the American efforts to unravel the international Gordian knots. The healthy American society, which trusts in God, gives hope for the survival of humanity. However, will it persist to resist, as it has against terrorism, as against immoral agnostic storms of agnosticism?

The same image prevails throughout the world, with anarchic-liberalism and Islamic fundamentalism being two sides of the same coin. The first desires moral chaos for American society, while the other would like to kill every American.

Laozi

Once upon a time, some disciples asked their teacher, Laozi, "Who is the best man in the world?" Loazi didn't answer, so they pressed him further, "Is he a man loved by most people?"

Laozi replied this time, "No, he is not!"

After some time the discussion continued:
Is he a man loved by everyone?
No, he is not!
Is this man unloved by everyone?
No, he is not!
Who is he then?
He is the man who is loved by the good people and hated by the evil ones!

Is It Time? Or Not Yet?

The voices of religious extremism and liberal anarchy spread the flames of Holy War around the world. The international community does not take it seriously, and many refuse to accept and understand the USA's position. Only humor is serious to some political leaders.

The world seems like an idyllic image of democratic blindness creating *naive nations,* as much by those who try to oppose democracy through religion as those who promote democracy as a religion.

For a moment, it literally seems that every Islamic practitioner becomes a slave of fanaticism. The demonstrations all over the world give this impression. Jihad has become the most important expression of Islam in the Islamic world.

This is a key point of Islamic behavior. They all pray for it. They build their security on the words of their prophet, who promised them victory.

Some media experts explain that the only difference between an extremist and a moderate believer is one disputable question: Is it time to kill my neighbor or not!

This could mean that those who answer "yes" are terrorists, but the rest are also preparing themselves for the same task. At first glance, it could maybe be seen as a humorous aspect of our time, but it isn't funny. It is more serious than many comprehend.

Long ago, their prophet called upon them to kill Jews and Christians. He obliged his followers to do this, even to their extermination. The extremists believe this command is eternal! Many therefore think their mission is to kill, with them just being holy warriors.

The opinion that Jihad is based on this misunderstanding of the Islamic scriptures becomes irrelevant at this moment.

From an intelligent point of view, it is not rational to interpret ancient words so literally in modern times. However, if someone does do this, humanity needs to find a serious solution. The answer needs to be strong, prompt, and rational.

This is not a call to start another crusade. It is an appeal to the UN to forbid the radical misuse of any holy scripture.

Patron of America

Wednesday March 19, 2003

Today is the feast of Saint Joseph, Jesus' stepdad. He is the patron saint of Belgium, Canada, and my little Croatia, as well as some other countries.

I live in Belgium, but I intend to travel to Canada as soon as possible. I always keep Croatia in my heart, however. Every day, I visit her great islands, albeit just in thought.

Today, I would like to express how I love the USA like my homeland. I can see its patron is God.

At the moment, I am in the church of Saint Michael the Archangel, the traditional patron of Brussels. He is the patron of armies and the nobility, as well as my own family. I will attend Mass, and this is a special evening of prayer for the time.

Saint Michael is the Duke of The Heavenly Army, and his task is to defeat the evil spirits. I have the impression his soldiers conduct this mission in the heavens, while the American forces try to follow it on Earth.

Is this the eve of the clash of civilizations? Many Muslims provoke the Jihad, and many Christians are ready to respond, but some pray for peace, such as in this church.

I have already learned how to pray for even my enemies. The armies prepare themselves for a new conflict. Our hearts sense that it is the last day of peace before the apocalyptic events begin! I pray from my heart:
O' Saint Michael the Archangel, fight for us Against
evil and devilish ambushes,
Be to us our shelter.
Then God command
And to you, Duke of the heavenly host, I humbly pray.
Then Satan, and the other evil spirits,
Who travel around the world to destroy souls,

End in Hell by the power of God!

During my own country's war for freedom, I used to fight and pray. Today, I plead for the liberty of the world. It is my way of supporting justice.

I'm maybe not a hero myself, but I benefit from some family history. One of my grandfathers sacrificed himself for the USA, and President Roosevelt posthumously awarded him the Medal of Honor, the highest American distinction for bravery. Today, however, those who pray are like heroes, because true believers have become rarer than heroes.

Tomorrow is Thursday. I remember one rainy Thursday some years ago. I had lost my manuscript about my past war times. I prayed, in vain apparently, the prayer of *Jabez,* which I had written on the first page of that French text.

I was too sad and disappointed to do anything other than desperately follow Providence through my rainy steps. Protecting myself from the rain, I by chance found myself on the trail of my family.

I stood by a cinema and noticed there was a showing of my favorite movie of that year, *Pearl Harbor.* My grandfather perished there as one of human pearls of Pearl Harbor, pearls we will find in the House of God one day.

Once again, America is forced to step up. I feel that God needs heroes more than prayers this time.

The entire world media is counting down the minutes before the President's ultimatum to the Iraqi government expires. Tomorrow will without doubt be a historical Thursday.

I trust in God that my Archangel prayer will protect every word of the diary I begin writing now.

WAR DIARY FROM BRUSSELS

A Baptism of Fire for the 21st Century

3/20/2003

It is the early hours of the morning, and I feel like a night watchman. It's 3:25 am as I listen to BBC Radio London.

It is time for a baptism of fire for the 21st century. It seems like Caesar has crossed the Rubicon! Mr. Bush is going to Baghdad.

I remember 9/11/2001. Many people feared that nothing would be the same again and started to imagine a dark vision of the future.

There are special broadcasts on every TV channel. Bush manifests the dignity of a misunderstood leader. The expression in his face speaks spiritually about a very rare personality in contemporary politics. He is more intriguing than many of his predecessors and the current leaders of the world.

He emotionally understands our time, yet he cannot find understanding among the majority of the misinformed population. The future will comprehend him, though.

Saddam tells his story. Some commentators remark that he waffles like Bin Laden through cassettes. Jihadist phrases connect them together.

It's like a soap opera. Many claim to speak in the name of God, but only those who are on His side will be blessed.

The Americans begin their first military operations like surgeons. The Iraqis respond by launching some missiles into Kuwait. The general impression is that these missiles are not capable of hitting anywhere near their intended targets. It seems the Iraqis need to learn more about guidance systems.

Their rockets fall down like Bedouins dying before an oasis in an unknown desert. They do not see their mistakes.

Today, masks take the first place of interest. It is a dominant decoration for the media. It spreads fears because of poison gases and panics because of SARS.

It is obvious that all the analysts paint their faces with the makeup of WMDs. They are either too confused or too clever, but they are always separated from reality because of their limited experience.

In spite of numerous wars, men act like parrots at the beginning of each new conflict. There is the flourishing of experts. They know everything, yet they say nothing.

New faces in the role of sages try to explain things that people do not understand. However, it is not possible to be an expert on war. Nobody can skillfully answer all our questions. I personally feel that the theory and practice of it are as distant as the Iraqi rockets are from their targets.

Some media outlets inform us well, but there is always error when understanding their comments. Maybe it is because I don't understand some mentalities, so I need to make do with a literal interpretation.

Strange forces sometimes spread fear in abundance, but I believe the American head is cool.

It is always important to mention who is an ally of whom. The Americans try to give the impression that many allies support them, but everyone knows that they do not need anybody else. Some skeptical experts even go so far as to deny they have any firm allies other than Britain.

Sometimes I exaggerate, but it's only to express a hint of humor. It is time to go to sleep and try to catch a dream, but I cannot because I am thinking...

***

It's now the afternoon. Coalition troops have crossed over the border between Iraq and Kuwait.

In the evening, I manage to shield myself from an explosion of news. The center of Baghdad is blazing like an Olympic torch, but the information is not so bright.

Scud missiles over Kuwait die in the air with a kiss of death. If the Iraqis, by some chance, manage to launch their rockets toward intended or unintended targets, there is always time for the sophisticated American technology to prove its superiority. It knows what to do.

These "Patriots" are like guardian angels. These missiles discourage all American enemies. Everything is ready, and maybe Reagan's Star Wars vision will be realized one day, at least if humanity survives the Holy War.

I am not a friend of any weapons. God save us from them! Our imagination is stretched to the limits, because the reality resembles the magical stories of the famous Harry Potter! I turn off the TV.

BBC Radio London tries to get answers for some issues. Do the Iraqis have the capacity to use WMDs? It seems they also have some suspicions about the American evidence that the dictator still holds that evil. However, we know he used them during his war against Iran.

It is a dammed river on the globe. Only a refugee can understand refugees.

I remember how the Desert Storm of 1991 was an overture to the Yugoslav wars of the next seven years. I will never forget the blind reaction of the international community.

It was on the wrong side for much of that time, and there were consequently hundreds of thousands of deaths and millions of refugees. Although winner, my Croatia, was one of the victims of the corrupt UN.

It was a painful experience for my soul, and nothing can erase it, at least not for a long time. Nobody can tell me anything about moral European standards. It always needs more lessons.

I understand that some politicians need to see the biblical star of the Magi before they can follow the truth. The UN has not organized itself to act together toward the salvation of the world.

According to biblical research, Eden existed somewhere within the borders of Iraq.

Today, it is very easy to be a prophet and say, "God created man there, and now it's time to destroy him there." Somebody might have thought the same thing ten years ago, so we should probably take all the apocalyptic stories with a pinch of salt.

Some people enjoy heralding the end of the world. Sometimes it even seems serious, because during a war, every day can feel like an apocalypse for the people involved.

I do not listen to these modern oracles. Only one true apocalyptic prophet exists for all times, and he is Saint John, the writer of the Apocalypse. Nobody knows, but some believe he did not die and is preparing, through wars, the way for the Second Coming of Jesus Christ. I would like to believe this, but I hope Jesus will come one day regardless.

According to the Apocalypse, before He returns, there will be a time of great destruction. The modern prophets see this image through a mirror of the current times. All their stories are merely metaphors from scared minds.

The Book of Revelation demands from us a perfect key that was lost in past times. We are not clever enough to speak on that level anymore. I talk about the evangelical Apocalypse rather than apocalypses.

I remember a pretty American girl; she understood the Apocalypse as a marvel of God's word to realize the Mormons' plans. I would like to see her again and understand more this time!

I would also like to see Tara, a second child of God I know, but the SARS virus prevented me from traveling to Canada. This time is not a friend of journeys anywhere. The world is very poor, and our own shadows become our fears.

So-called peaceful demonstrations continue all over the world. They make a noise, and it's a mess! I know among the masses, there are mixed apples and pears! I ask myself whether this is a question for Darwin or Michurin?

There is an eruption of evil that tries to catch up to the hand of God. The friends of the Jihad are out of control. It is just one image among the general prostitution of words.

They only cry in vain. They are like creatures from outside of time and space. Many dream of becoming Mujahidin. For these people, there is neither the future nor the present, except in their imaginations.

It is funny to point out, but everybody needs to take responsibility for what is happening around us. This is not a time for pretty proclamations. Americans realize that the key question is the questionable future.

The UN is not capable of accepting its leadership until humankind realizes the full measure of being human. Forced by circumstances, which others do not understand, America protects our civilization.

There is no choice this time. There is no peace without the force of the USA. This is so despite those who protest against the war and those who do not have the courage to speak the truth about terrorism. We can be afraid of the conflict, but it is our decision to make today or tomorrow, because it might be too late the day after tomorrow.

Anti-Americanism is a major reason for the culmination of wrathful demonstrations. Peace is relegated to the secondary reason. Reality is rational, but irrational moments are like chains around the neck and legs of our generation, which does not want peace in the name of peace.

Smoke and flame have created the most attractive picture of this day. It burns in the south of Iraq. Basra is a puzzle for the British.

"If love does not burn, let the crude oil burn" or "Make love not war!" I write down the spirit of the so-called peacemakers' words.

This time, I think there are more antiwar inscriptions around us, more nonsense among us, although I respect their romantic expressions. Naivety is like suicide!

Somebody threw a Molotov cocktail toward the American Embassy in Brussels. The police then caused panic using water cannons! I feel that many others need a cold shower as well. Al-Qaeda shows how it has many supporters in this part of Belgium.

A misguided bomb hit an oil refinery inside Iran, near the northern border with Iraq. It is a chance mistake, or maybe it is a measure of admonition toward another member of the Axis of Evil. Regardless, the Americans apologized to Iran.

Sometimes, something is out of order, and it will cause something to happen, whether it is bringing freedom to Iraq or the twilight of the clash of civilizations...

First Day of Spring

3/21/2003

Around 30 oil wells are burning. There are fears that all the Iraqi oil fields could burst into flame.

Hundreds of Iraqi soldiers wave white flags. It seems that cities are surrendering without resistance. Tanks rumble through the Iraqi desert with the speed of a fox toward Baghdad.

The first Coalition troops are dead. A helicopter crashed, and there was a muddle of information about the number of victims. Three of them were English brigadiers, and it was an accident. Another two soldiers perished on the battlefield.

On the Iraqi side, many are dead, injured, or captured, but all are frightened. The Iraqi people tremble like their soil.

It's two days, and Saddam's residence already seems like the puffed-up smoke from his pipe. According to some reports, he is dead or injured. This would mean that the first bombs determined his fate, but doubts are cast over the reports.

Demonstrations are continuing in Brussels and all over the world. Arabs and Europeans shout out together that Bush is an assassin. Without doubt, many among them are killers.
Belgian TV interviews children in the first year of an elementary school, even the youngest from a kindergarten. Journalists look for reinforcements for their antiwar viewpoints.

The children prove that Bush is a bad boy who intends to hurt the Iraqi children. Somebody obviously thinks that toddlers make the best war experts.

Pride, fear, and misunderstanding, mixed with feelings of anti-Americanism, show the true face of the empty democratic conscience.

Education line by line and section by section is the weakness of modern intelligence.

The gentlemen have disappeared!

It is a form of brainwashing! The police fight delirious youths in front of the American Embassy in Brussels. It is a consequence of the retarded reactions of their chiefs.

Two hundred Iraqis fight for the British forces. Iraq denies the massive surrendering of its soldiers, who then continue to support their enemy.

The Iraqi government spokesman gave a sarcastic commentary, probably because Britain has fewer troops than America. This man is already making us laugh.

I notice some of his nebulous ideas: *"Bush is a gangster. He is Al Capone. America is a gangster superpower. Iraq is the superpower of the will,"* and so on. This was the set of meaningless phrases I heard today on BBC Radio London. Needless to say, he is a poor master of propaganda.

Today is the first day of the spring and the beginning of the end of the Iraqi events.

This day gives the impression that the war could be over soon, faster than anybody thought possible.

It seems that among the demonstrators, there is no one able to lead them in an intellectual manner. It is just a street full of people. I see mainly schoolchildren, lost teachers, stray workers, tramps, Mujahedin, and some decoration from the Belgian extreme left. They are many, but they are like sheep without a shepherd.

Some popular politicians are sometimes there, but only as further proof of the general madness. I forgot to mention the very charming female figures with their children and cakes. They promote their magical recipes!

Brussels shouts in vain, and it only creates many new demons.

The Americans have arrested thousands of protestors in the USA because of their violent antiwar attitudes.

Peace is a great challenge. Some naive people really think that somebody wants the war. Americans do not understand Americans. Evil is the same thing everywhere.

It would be understandable if somebody demonstrated against Saddam's abuse of power. However, this is not a fashionable expression of personality—the trend is to be against Bush.

Democratic liberal narcissism asks for satisfaction with the popular side. Everybody knows that the mass always leads toward hell, but it seems that many like it.

Peace can exist in the world only if humanity continues to fight permanently for it everywhere, even when it is not popular to be a cowboy.

If the would-be politicians agreed to follow the street chaos, the end of our civilization could begin right this moment. Most of the population is too blind to see their blindness. It is our modern apocalyptic ailment.

Bush shows the last moral democratic force of mind to clear a path to the future. With American steps, the light of understanding will take a new position to wash up the hopes of the snobbish world. Iraq probably did not deserve to be the only target, though.

The unconscious victims of the actual situation are the governments that encourage demonstrations in the name of so-called peace. They go hand in hand with the jihadists in causing general confusion.

Imperious manners stay in the dreams of many.

God save us from their peace! They are not ready to accept responsibility. They take part in the creation of the dream of a universal

Islamic state. They are not aware that when they do so, they start a history of collaboration with Evil.

The world's Masonry does not understand our time either. Bush is a different builder. It is his advantage, because he is not burdened by wicked imagination. He might be making some mistakes, but his heart is clean. This is not the case with others.

Rational minds refuse to listen to anymore of the Russian–French fables. Democracy needs to be more than the combination of different interests. This time, there is no compromise based on a wise, democratic solution, because the enemy is irrational.

The French government surprises many, but not many French people. It is a nation that has lost the colors of its identity. It is on the way to becoming the first European Islamic state. Its democracy can no longer be a beacon for the rest of the world. It needs a new French revolution to put things in order!

An anti-American hysteria flourishes among Belgians. So, many think that Bush is a religious extremist. It serves the media coverage by using people who would never say something like that about the Mujahedin.

It goes like this: *"Bush has very Calvinist attitudes. Calvinist philosophy has cruel moral standards subordinated to fate and considers pleasure wrong or unnecessary"* and so on.

Nobody denounces Islamic movements as dangerous. Sometimes extremists are on the cross, but it is always within the frame of extremism.

Hysteria is not just a consequence of misunderstanding but also an eruption of fear. This is Belgium. As regards Germany, I have to say I understand the Germans because of their history. It is probably best for them to remain in a neutral position for as long as possible.

Sometimes it is good to enjoy some sarcastic comments. Germans, as we know, always lose wars, so it is better for the coalition to be without some allies. Some say so. Do they really think so?

The extreme left all over the world try to use the new circumstances to make an unnatural division in the democratic body of our civilization. They make Bush and Blaire into hawks and compare them to Sharon, trying to attract the blind political populous to their so-called side of peace. They are red bastards.

In Belgium, they are open protectors of extreme Islamic movements. They need Muslims, not just as an electoral resource but also as a convenient means to create anarchy when it is necessary to protect their interests.

The American flag becomes a symbol of hate, as much among Europeans as Arabs. Its burning image has become an everyday sight.

Modern youths without identity easily accept the role of the wild character. There is no longer any measure of behavior as a balance between good and bad. It is a moral apocalypse, and war is always the consequence.

I'm no crusader, but I see the American Army as a ship working for the salvation of the world, and not just this time. Many Europeans do not discern the banners of peace from the inscriptions of animosity. I repeat: They walk together with those who shout out to their God as a leader of jihad. Europeans through their manifestations express very naive characters.

Where are their roots?

It is like a dance of moths around an anti-American lamp. At one of the Parisian railroad stations, there was found a trace of the poisonous ricin as a gift for everybody.

Terrorists try to destroy Christian civilization. Some support them with the naivety of democracy.

I try to make my up mind, to form a conclusion, and to discover a reason why Europe is incapable of recognizing the real danger of Islamism.

Under each extremist boot, we can read a bloody message: *We are on the way to spread Islam.* It means that they are Mujahedin, and their task is to either convert or kill. It does not digress. It is their holy path, the madness of a Holy War. They act according to their conscience.

One year ago on Christmas Eve, in Bosnia and Herzegovina in the heart of Europe, an Islamic fanatic enters the home of a catholic family and kills them with a machinegun. In the European media, this passes like an ordinary traffic accident.

Maybe the Croats who live there are not worthy of attracting attention because of their Christian roots. Nevertheless, there among them exists one of the last oases of moral European Christianity. Europe renounces its roots.

The European Masonry prefer Islam, but they promote something worse. This is the obliged bisexual behavior as a political option. They are masters of relativism. It is the ideology of the Antichrist. Liberally, terror (literally) places itself as the only democratic landmark.

In some European countries, it becomes like an obliged political direction, and they export it all over the world. Belgium is on its way to becoming one of the first strange democracies of the world. I cannot believe that God will allow it, unless Belgium really does deserve something like this.

The south of Iraq lies under an ever-growing curtain of smoke that describes the future. Meanwhile, the Iraqi extremists try to prevent other Iraqis from surrendering.

Tony Blair declares that nobody has ever fought like the British troops. He knows his job.

The Dictator on TV

3/22/03

The Europeans claim that America is a nation with a need for confrontation. Meanwhile, Iraq demands that the UN Security Council stop the aggression.

The hundreds of civilian casualties appear as a warning to all. One source says that most of these are merely injured, but whether killed or wounded, it is always a tragedy. This is the primary reason why I hate war.

In spite of all this, I have the impression that the American military operations are conducted with surgical precision. I compare this to some other less discriminating wars. However, it can never take away honor from the innocent ones. Although war is sometimes unavoidable, it cannot serve perfect justice all the time.

Our fight for goodness often creates horror on the way to realizing its objectives.

Both the Turks and the Kurds deny reports that Turkish forces have crossed the northern Iraqi border. Ankara undoubtedly intends to benefit from the war. For them, it is not acceptable that the liberty of the Kurds might come one day.

Tanks continue to hurry toward Baghdad, and obstacles present few serious problems. The forces advance at a great pace, surprising their Iraqi friends.

Journalists describe Iraq using comments and TV pictures like hellfire preachers. It seems the reality is worse than any nightmare. I feel some are exaggerating it, but who knows? It could be just an innocent taste of what we could experience in the future.

The Americans do not need long to assess the results of their bombings. The fire is permanent.

The demonstrations continue to draw attention. I prefer to stay at home, well away from the single-minded multitude outside. If I am there, by chance, I am not among them; I merely pass beside them to catch an outline of the reality of it all with my eye-camera. The TV channels often distort their reports to attach undue importance to things.

I always respect rivers of sweat, but this time, I cannot share the sea of misunderstandings and solidarity with the jihadists. I pray for peace more intensively.

Many do not understand what is happening around us. It's not because of Bush. It's not because of the crude oil. It does not have anything to do with big business. It's not because somebody wants the clash of civilizations. It is a question of life or death. I know I'm not exaggerating!

If there are people who want the war, we can find them among the anti-American demonstrators. The extremists and their friends are on the same mission. It seems like a paradox, but it's true. It is the real face on the street.

Of course, there is confusion there because of so many interests. We can meet sincere people there as well, but they're also very naive. It is an image of so-called peacemakers this time. I am sorry!

There are Kurdish victims who still support the Iraqi regime, and these people are damned forever. Opportunities arise from time to time, but they choose not to change their fate. It is a poor Kurdish destiny.

There is also the other side of the Kurdish coin. A dream about an independent state now seems like it may be a feasible vision one day, but it is still just a dream. However, some Kurds are forgetting to dream, because not all of them are happy to be free.

It seems Turkey lurks ready to steal the fruit of the Kurdish nightmare and enforce its domination over them. Many Kurds—who live as minorities around the borders between Iraq, Turkey and Iran—know their history, a story of genocide during the Ottoman occupation, probably the cruelest empire the human race has created. We can imagine the Kurdish opinion about the Turks.

I hope that America watches the situation closely. I am not so sure anymore that Turkey is a sincere ally of the USA, especially considering Kurdistan.

A proverb among the Balkans says that nobody can believe a Turk, even if he is your brother. It is a consequence of 600 years of constant combat with them.

I am a Croat, and I do not hate the Turks despite our turbulent history with them. However, if I do speak about them, I always remember the Battle of Krbava Field in 1493. It took hundreds of thousands of Croats.

However, the Ottomans never occupied Croatia, which was *the antimurale christianitatis (Latin for the Bulwark of Christianity).* However, they could still rule over the whole of Europe one day, together with their Islamic brothers. This would happen not because they could become a great military power, but rather because the Christians could disappear spiritually as much as physically.

Maybe it could be a democratic empire, but is it in the interests of Europe? Europeans have not learned much from their painful history.

For many nations, the Turkish terror is just a tragic history, but it is an everyday nightmare for the Kurds.

Turkey insists on making itself a part of Europe so it can join the European Union. America supports this irrational plan, and I am disappointed with them in this case. If this were ever realized, it would be the first step in dividing Europeans. It would be a great thing if we were ripe for that union, but democracy needs more time to realize some idyllic ideas.

This is just my opinion, although I know that hundreds of millions of others think the same. It is not our revenge; it is just our message.

If the USA tries to form the EU like a pancake, I can understand why, but I am European, so I do not like it sometimes. I am afraid that America will lose two allies in the case of this unnatural marriage, but the way things are in modern Europe, nobody will be surprised.

The birds already repeat that it is like Mexico becoming part of the USA. Sometimes Chirac (the French President) knows how to express what his nation feels to be a danger.

Saddam has suddenly appeared on Iraqi TV. It tries to portray him as the leader of jihadists. I saw one frightened face with a forced smile. He said that he is alive and that the enemy lies again. He tries to invoke Arab sympathies with fiery words. He asks for their help, yet he refused to speak with them just a few days ago.

Nobody can change some Muslims. He knows that, so he speaks as he does. Many respect neither force nor reality. It is their cross, and many will be there.

Saddam flies on his TV wings while the rumors about his death continue to spread. He is like a dreamer. Some people indulge their imaginations with his exaggerations, and this is just what he wishes for.

Trendy experts try to say that it might not have really been Saddam, because it is well known that he has look-alikes. I hope that he has not cloned himself. Maybe his speech was filmed a long time before.

It's all rumors. Saddam is dead! Many say this, not just rumormongers. Many don't believe it, and nobody can prove it either way. I feel like it is a kind of psychological war.

It seems that the American Apache helicopter has had its famous reputation tarnished. It was an accident, but there are too many accidents happening there. If it really is this bad, it reflects poorly on the safety of the Apache. Then again, I appreciate that not every helicopter accident involves an Apache.

It becomes clear that some things are out of the Coalition's control. American troops face the first troubles.

Thousands of Iraqi soldiers decorate themselves with improvised white flags. An Iraqi government representative portrays soldiers as civilians. It's all lies and smiles, while the Pentagon tries to conquer the world using true information.

The pocket of resistance in Basra provokes the British forces there. Fanatics from the whole of the Islamic world try through fear to regain control over the inhabitants, prolonging their agony.

Civilians suffer, and the Americans endeavor to open a corridor for humanitarian aid.

Pope John Paul II is very concerned about the future of humanity. If other world leaders would follow his example, paradise could be returned to Earth.

He has his reasons, but his dignity is unquestionable. He trusts in Jesus with an open heart, more so than anybody before him. His God died for the salvation of the human race and didn't ask any man to fight others for him. I understand that God has no need of jihadists.

He demands responsibility from all the players. He invites the whole world to keep the peace, not just the Americans. He tries to put France, Germany, Russia, and China in order. He is afraid of the reason why the members of UN Security Council are divided.

Humanity owes him a debt of gratitude for all he has done for world peace. More respect accorded to his words would lead to more love among us.

This time, no one alone can do that much. However, I think the Vatican administration is able to take some decisive steps, such as reorganizing the UN and giving them a moral dimension as a means against particular interests. I think President Bush could be the best partner for that.

Some weeks before the war, it was very shameful for any democrat to look powerless. The powerbrokers buzzed around the world to gain a majority of the UN Security Council through the divided interests of its members.

I do not want to present myself as an infallible war expert, but I refuse to believe the opinions of many. This is not because of my five years of experience with war, but rather because of the political childishness of some old heads.

The TV repeats its repetitions again, so I turn it off.

Judas's Price

3/23/2003

The Americans are nearing Baghdad.

Iraqi representatives meanwhile declare that Iraq has lured the enemy into a trap. The Pentagon denies the possibility, though.

Iraqis try to spread lies and create confusion among the Coalition. It is the only new sensation for the Arab media.

It seems as much fear as it is lies. Simple people and their political leadership manifest the signs of panic. The country is without a serious defense strategy, and this becomes more evident each day.

Fierce fighting continues on the outskirts of the town of Umm Quasar, situated near the border with Kuwait. The BBC speaks about the consolidation of Coalition troops as the Iraqis try to do something.

The Americans have downed a British fighter jet. The most sophisticated missile system in the world has been misused.

It could be a sign of a new diversion!

Then one marine, a Muslim among the American troops, conducts his own operation to kill marines. It is not friendly fire or an accident in the Kuwaiti desert. It is an act of a darkened mind. This is exactly why America fights its current battles.

Nobody comprehends, but everybody understands!

In Brussels, some people dream dreams about a European Army. They are trying to match the USA.

It's a paradox that the peacemakers look at themselves through a military force. I think that the strayed liberal heads are just dreaming about power over the USA, so they can spread their anarchic ideology there and create a new, controlled world order.

Somebody is always responsible or not responsible for something. It depends from which point of view we want to tackle anything today. Sometimes the best comment is no comment.

The Iraqis have destroyed two American tanks and killed one soldier. Some 15 marines are also injured, while some others are missing in action. In the battle for Nasiriyah, it is possible to discern a first sign of an organized resistance.

Two British pilots, victims of friendly fire from American forces, fell into the river Tigris. The Iraqis shot at them like vipers.

In the TV images, everybody can see Iraqi soldiers without a sense of soldier's dignity, especially not toward other soldiers.

An euphoric mentality and a primitive soul go together hand in hand.

The Arab TV broadcasts a cruel show with prisoners of war.

New fires dance around Basra.

Bush warns the American people that the war could take more time than anybody originally thought.

Nasiriyah becomes the center of attention. There were a hundred dead Iraqis, although Baghdad denies it. Some marines have been killed or captured. The war moves on to a higher level.

It is a bombardment of news, and I'm not always sure I can follow it in a clear chronological line.

The TV shows pictures of the humiliation and suffering of some American prisoners of war. Nobody accepts this with any understanding except for the Islamic media. It seems that cruelty is popular with them.

The USA asks for the application of the Geneva Convention.

Some commentators express the opinion that the Iraqis will suppress their fears and start to fight seriously. However, I know this would only show traits of a suicidal character.

Some Americans believe that America needs revenge, so they threaten to block the reconstruction of Iraq after the war if it continues to break the standards for the reasonable treatment of prisoners.

Tony Blair is again impressed with the courage of his troops. He disputes any doubts and says everything is going according to plan.

TV BF broadcasts an unusual report about the citizens of Baghdad allegedly distinguishing between Europeans and their governments, so everybody can walk freely about the city.

I'm sorry, but Europeans are not ready to commit suicide. It is too naive a TV message, although I can imagine some reporters pander to their Iraqi hosts so they can continue to work safely.

Fear is an unacceptable censor. It is like words far removed from the facts or even just plain lies. I try to piece together the images of the battlefield and everyday life.

For Iraqis, their mentality is their main enemy. The irrational minds among them spread messages for other irrational minds worldwide. Illusions are the first place of interest.

Some years ago, a young Iraqi woman tried to convince me that Iraqis are not Arabs; they're just Iraqis. I understand that some do not like being Arabs, but I may be wrong.

I was afraid they were like the Bosnian Muslims, who changed their five national names five times in just 50 years. This shows that nationality is not that significant to Islam.

I would like to make clear some divisions among Muslims, and it is probably very important to understand them. For the moment, however, I only feel my great wish to travel. There are some people I remember with nostalgia.

In spite of the circumstances, I try to respect my reasons. I enjoy writing my diary. It is a good opportunity to pray to God and change our habits before he punishes the Arabs or any one of us.

The Iraqi government representative answered some questions in his usual undiplomatic style. He tries to be funny, but he is rather like a puppet on stage. Concerning the Geneva Convention, he said that Iraq prefers to apply Islamic law toward prisoners of war.

He is the minister of information, but he is like the weather forecast, never correct, especially not about the future. It is too easy to recognize the direction of the clouds and winds in his mind.

Many enjoy listening to his lies, but I'm not sure that it can help Iraq.

He refuses all critics and tries to express feelings of offended national pride because of questions about the TV broadcasts constituting prisoner abuse. The Geneva Convention irritates him.

In defense, he said that Iraq is a nation of great history, putting forward physics and arithmetic as its contributions. He points out that the Iraqi side respects humanity, while the Bush forces are, as he literally said, "simple savages."

His phrases speak much about him, but they speak first about his role on this improvised stage for jihad. He is far away from the superiority he would like to show. It is just boasting.

It is true that the history of the Iraqi land (which was not always called Iraq) is a fantastic story. Today, however, it is just a fanatical tale. It is important to point out that the greatest of Iraq's past achievements occurred before the coming of Islamic culture. Islam has created a marginalized nation, which expresses its magnanimity only through the suicidal manners of holy warriors.

The Islam of the jihadists renounces all cultural expressions and traditions that existed before it. The two grand monuments of Buddha in Afghanistan are a recent example of such fundamentalism (or, more accurately, vandalism).

A Serbian war analyst on Radio Free Europe is a friend to some Iraqi generals. This demonstrates the friendship between two devilish nations. He has too much respect for Iraqis. He said that they are ready to fight to the last man. He tries to be a moderate person, but he cannot escape his own skin.

I recognize his mentality of megalomania, and therein lays the recipe to realize an advantage in anything the Serbs occupy. He is one of the Serbian academics who openly follow their motto of *lying is a means that has saved Serbs throughout their painful history* (meaning the six hundred years of slavery under Turks). I am not sure this experience can help Saddam, but maybe it will help the Kurds.

I feel that the victims of irrationality get satisfaction by tasting their lost dreams in the depths of their friend's imagination. I say this without any offence to his professionally integrity.

I sense that he cannot forget the capitulation of Kosovo (forced by American air strikes). Friends sometimes speak about us clearer than we can comprehend.

Pockets of resistance, caused by the suicidal ways of fanatics, are the biggest obstacle preventing the Coalition from conquering Iraqi cities. The superiority of the American weapons is so impressive that their enemy has no choice other than to hold up the white flag. However, some still enjoy being martyrs.

Iraqi TV is repeating movies about Tito, the former Yugoslav dictator. He is one of Saddam's idols. The Iraqis tell legends about him, and to them he is an invincible prince on a white horse. Tito, however, was a cruel warrior and an atheist. He would have had the jihadists all locked in prison.

Today, Saddam wears the mask of a holy warrior to maintain his authority, but he only tries because he wants to be a mirror of his idol. Tito becomes a saint!

His unlimited political power, his skill in warfare (cruel as it was), his practical political understanding of the world, and his luxury and many marriages are some of Tito's traits. It is clear that Saddam and Tito maybe share some of these, but the political wisdom and especially the skill at warfare have stayed far away from the Iraqi.

Maybe I have it wrong, because the Yugoslav dictator imagined a national notion of Muslims in Bosnia and Herzegovina to conquer his enemies. Saddam tries to be a better Muslim to obtain friends and destroy his enemy. In spite of all this, I'm not sure Tito would like to help Saddam with his current plight.

It sometimes seems that journalists enjoy wars, yet many times, it is obvious that wars do not like them. TV Lloyd has lost a man.

Saddam has proclaimed that the Coalition will not leave Iraq as live men. He has promised his soldiers $30,000 for every head from an enemy soldier.

An account from the Gospel says that Judas was given 30 pieces of silver to betray Jesus. This was the Jews' price for the Messiah's head. At first sight, Saddam's reward for American heads is a different thing.

As it says in the news of joy (the Gospel), Judas committed suicide. Every day, the fanatics in Iraq do the same.

Some American soldiers die like Jesus did, in the cruelty of fate, but the victory is for them as it was for Him. Their destinies are always both proud and poor. The American role of the Messiah (the resurrection of democracy) becomes the news of joy for Iraqis.

There is no freedom for the people without this painful, bloody experience.

Key of Ashes

3/24/2003

At dawn, I turn off the TV and the radio. I'm trying to create silence in my soul. I would like to put all my thoughts into the ashes of dreams.

At noon, my dreams are replaced with new TV images. Certain channels are unbearable, like always.

TV BF is interviewing children again. I appreciate neither this style of journalism nor the color of the children's language. The pupils speak more about their teachers than about their own vigor. It is like an instructive virus in the collective spirit.

It is a misuse of innocence to express anti-Americanism like this, and it borders on being criminal. Somebody needs to protect children from the abuse of these journalists. It is such an irony of democracy.

I dispute any explanation for the abuse of children in the name of any objective around us.

Children make up the largest group of victims in our modern times. At the moment, I have the impression that somebody made a coalition combining all of America's enemies with various kinds of pedophiles.

The ignorance of intellect manipulates emotions.

I would like if all that I wrote was just a slip of the pen. I would like to go to sleep again. I would like to change reality.

Suddenly, one dream urges me to put aside the TV images. I am overwhelmed with remembrance. I wonder as it plays on.

Light leads me to a grave. It is like a hillock made from terracotta. I have a question. The tomb is open, and the clay around the body is cracked. The person is alive.

I see the beautiful yet serious face of a young woman. I know it is one of our ancestors, foremother Eva. She looks at me with her calm eyes. It is an expression of surprise. She just wishes to see who receives the precious gift of her appearance.

Then she disappears.

I'm confused. I think about this heavenly message as if it is the most serious question I need to understand.

Maybe it's a consequence of my sleepless nights, or maybe it's my belief that God's wrath comes over the Garden of Eden once more.

This could be an explanation for my dream, but I cannot accept any suggestions at the moment. Nevertheless, I feel a need to explain it.

Once upon a time, somewhere out there in modern-day Iraq, there was our fatherland. Today the rumble of war moves our ancestors' bones again. My soul feels their graves in the depths of the ground and trembles with them as bombs explode above them.

It seems that Evil wishes to prevent the time of resurrection.

It bears the message for the time being. I believe that each tomb understands our time, better than anybody. My soul received the bliss of enlightenment from reading traces of the dreams of the first men of Eden.

Our civilization has the key of ashes, but the key of life is the power of God. We go astray. Our fathers reproach us, because they would like to see their children only in love.

Today, I only want to dream. I want to move all the colors of the media to the background.

The media try to present Bush as a war criminal. They question all of his words.

Some even describe the President of the USA as the biggest evil and the greatest enemy of humanity. Some Europeans are among them, and this makes me ashamed that I'm European.

I compare his character with the greatest political virtuosos of America. He deserves to be among them, not for the war but for fairness. The war is the consequence of those who attacked him. He just acts in self-defense and protects the whole world. Whether the war is the only solution could be questioned, but his noble intentions cannot.

Some people are incapable of thinking on a moral plane, so they are unable to comprehend his decisions. For instance, he is the only man endowed with enough power to return the UN to the ethical roots of its founders. If he doesn't do this, no one ever will, because the world goes astray toward its end.

People do not like anybody who tries to correct their mistakes against their will, so our future belongs to the apocalyptic expressions of our ignorance.

If America acted like the anti-American governments, we would all quickly experience a general hell.

Certain politicians live in the clouds of their imaginations, and they are not ready to sacrifice any of their luxury in the name of humanity. They see the world as a simple virtual game without moral rules. Therefore, they enjoy their personal image of its advanced democratic attitudes without fear (or fixed by fear) for the future.

For them, democracy is their religion. However, they are atheists in an agnostic service!

This is the bitterest taste for the lost European generation, as much for the dreams of democracy as for the idealism of human rights. They see only their pleasure.

Our future demands suffering from everybody. Idealism must be removed from egoism and anarchy. Everyone is responsible for peace and the quest for justice for all.

We need to point out the founding principle of the UN as our aim. It was moral.

It is the Oscars ceremony night, but the winners are not important this time. I would give all the awards to just one person. He is the master of my dream, mentioned above.

Saddam prays to God that Iraqi victory will come fast. Although he is an ordinary Sunnite, he speaks like a fanatic. For his conversion, he needs to be grateful to America. I think that Islam is not the main reason for fanaticism in Arabs but rather their mentality.

Sixty-two Iraqi soldiers have died in the last 24 hours.

American helicopters continue to fall down.

Some of the Oscar winners protest severely against the war. One says, *"Mister Bush, shame on you forever."* He really is an actor! Although he has barely learned the political alphabet, he is able to show his stance.

Actors often cannot step out of their vocation. When they do sometimes, they are usually like fish out of water. It is typically emotional for the Oscars.

I enjoy the beauty of some of the women. For a moment, I have no interest in their political opinions.

Some maybe think that because they are actors like Ronald Reagan, they could be a good president, better even than he was.

It's true that there is a need to implant some moral traits into the leaders of the world, but this is not limited to them—it is a general moral crisis.

Many speak without measure, because the human being puts itself (through selfishness) before all virtue. Interest is God, or God is the interest. There is not a first place for God among people of the democratic world. Although many do everything in the name of God, it seems that true Divinity is banished from our planet. Therefore, many devils govern as gods.

The time being (not just the Oscars' night) is the time of the image. It is a trend among celebrities to be some kind of a corrective personality to label others (without arguments). To speak about the war is more popular with actors than playing a role in any movie.

After the death of some marines, some journalists become an easy prey for propaganda. It suddenly seems that the Iraqi Army attained the status of the world's fourth greatest military power. I note that their profession loses its dignity.

Horror creates more horror.

The Pentagon tries to explain a misunderstanding, with information coming from different sources. It is a quarrel between journalists in the base at Qatar.

The American media did not broadcast the footage of the humiliated US soldiers. It was the recommendation, or maybe the order, of the Pentagon to the media.

Koffi Annan, Secretary-General of the UN, has refused the Iraqi request for a ceasefire.

BBC Radio London shows the first signs of anxiety. They are not open supporters of either side. They try to be objective, but can they really?

Many people are worried. The general opinion about Iraq changes its colors. The casualties warn everybody to take the war more seriously.

The media continues to explain Iraq's past, exploiting the topic put forward by the Iraqi government representative.

The history of nations, without exception, is a permanent up-and-down process. In the days of yore, Iraq was the first of all the old (and now dead) civilizations, which the West very well appreciates. However, as we know, many Muslims look on this as an old age of demons.

The Iraqi regime is a moral zero, and it does not deserve as much respect. It has had its time, and now it has to go to the trash bin of time. They cannot justify themselves using ancient history.

The parrots on TV repeat the words of Saddam, "Be patient! Victory is coming."

It would be better to say the truth, as much about the past as about the future of his regime, rather than talking about the history of Iraq. Iraqis suffer and live their time separated from the reality of democratic nations.

Saddam cudgels one's brain to improvise some solution for himself.

He desperately catches up with the last chance. He could stop telling lies and save people from the war, but for him this is out of the question. He prefers to puff smoke out of his pipe.

Many Europeans defend the Iraqi side and disdain all what they think is going toward Bush's interests. Some old heads make a mask out of anti-Americanism, so they can be popular with the youths.

Indoctrination by the mistakes (through the media, etc.) of democratic idealism shows the superficial knowledge of many, journalists as much as ordinary people. They need to discern a way to sense the truth among the information.

Some believe the Masonry is backing Bush, misusing his sense of justice to realize their secret aims. This could be true, but he is not responsible for that.

However, it is a tragedy of our time that there is no serious opposition to the hidden elites. A world dictatorship is our destiny.

Some who intentionally act to offend America employ public opinion as a shelter for their activities. At the same time, they form it with their own attitude that everybody needs to be against the war. The masses cannot justify all their ignorance.

This war is more than a battle against Iraq. It is the lesser of two evils. It is prevention.

One group of Iraqi fanatics dance around an Apache helicopter like Native-American Apaches would beside their prey some hundreds of years ago. Euphoria is again the outline and highlight of primeval behavior.

It is more than a TV image this time. Is it just a simple revenge of destiny to the Americans because of their past cruelty to the Native Americans, as it is said? Of course, I like Indians!

Does the American helicopter need to change its beautiful name because it does not like cowboys? Maybe, it would be enough just to improve some of its technical characteristics. It is not only my feeling but also that of some Americans.

It resounds through Brussels every day: *"Bush is an assassin."*

I can listen to it in many different languages and in many different places. Because Arabs mainly speak French, it is usually this melody I hear. TV BF is my best tester.

English is misused as well. Dedications and inscriptions are mainly in English. There are numerous sentences in Arabic letters, but it is easy to get their meaning in any language.

Every day, the demonstrations remind me of a foxhunt out of season. In spite of it all, I can see the police take care in handling them.

One Belgian priest, a friend or just a person I know (I do not wish to offend him), seems like an exorcist when he goes to take part in the anti-war demonstrations. I know that everybody can see that many devils play there, but I am not sure that exorcism is his job. He never takes the Bible to such occasions!

He is always dressed like the peacemaker from the 60s and 70s of the last century. I am afraid he cannot forget the war in Vietnam. He was young then. Maybe he would like to be young again. He is too honest to be among others on the street, but he is there because he thinks that we need to prevent any war any way.

Yesterday, he asked me, *"Have you been to the demonstration?"* The rest of the conversation went as follows:

-No, I wasn't there.
-Why?
-I do not like it.
-Why?
-I support America.
-How can you support the war?
-I'm for peace.
-War is always bad.
-Yes, I know, but some things are sometimes worse.
-I don't like any war.
-I hate war too.

He is a very sincere man and very intellectual, but I am afraid he is too much of a political idealist. I saw disappointment in his eyes. I'm not sure that he understood me, because he looked at me like an exorcist.

The demons are on the other side sometimes, so I think the demonstrations are the best place for him, although he should take his Bible and cross in such circumstances.

I see two Mormon missionaries at a metro station. They observe an anti-American parade of young Muslims. The Mormons look at them like people from another planet. They do not like wars, but I'm not sure they like these protestors either.

Youths, as well as others, make up reasons for offending the USA and President Bush. On many foreheads, I can read the crossed-out word "Bush." It is trendy!

The anti-American graffiti of today are the favorite decoration of Brussels. I feel it is dirty, disgusting, and hysterical. It is directed without any dignity toward anybody or anything they do not understand.

The streets inspire the media, and the streets find more inspiration in the media.

Fashion is very important for every generation, but this one has been manipulated by the politicians, the media, and people with their own agendas. Fashion is a manipulation, and the manipulation is a fashion.

Europe loses its image of an old dame and becomes like a prostitute. I believe it is still the old dame, because no prostitute is too old. She adopted many children who do not love her.

Islamic ideologists worldwide preach very strongly that Muslims should form just one nation. For now, it's not that serious, but it could be realized one day. Most of the Islamic states make up the connected territory. However, it is a major objective of the jihadist plan to create a universal Islamic state.

They manifest their disproval. They are knitted in a cordon of noise from Jordan through Pakistan to Indonesia, from Egypt through Maghreb to Turkey, from the Balkans to Scandinavia. I see it go through Brussels like an identity parade every day.

Many refuse to see the general problem and recognize the building danger. Many support them, because they do not understand the political language of evil, despite many speaking it.

Everybody knows hate is like a virus. It kills the person bringing it, but others are also in jeopardy. Many are not conscious of their peril, because they are unaware of the apocalyptic mind. Therefore, they run the risk of doing something that seems very attractive at first sight.

Extremists prepare themselves for a collective suicide. It is the meaning of Jihad. It is the public opinion.

The same lament tries to gather the same hatred. They do not like America, because the American Army is an obstacle on the way of fanaticism. They shout out, "We are not cowards." They prove it with their suicide attacks.

Suicide is cowardice to the rational mind, but for them it is martyrdom. They provoke their governments, which are unable to do anything except scream together with them. This is the reason why they desperately seek to develop nuclear weapons.

If they ever had the power, they would destroy the USA in an instant. Many of them are simple metaphors of 9/11. I hope all fanatics will disappear like a loved but fleeting moment before they obtain that power.

I keep in mind the war in Bosnia and Herzegovina, and I remember the battle for Kosovo. I conclude that America is a big friend to the Islamic world. Extremists are their primary enemy, however, and I am afraid they do not deserve any friendship.

The animosity that terrorists create, and which defines them, needs to be recognized by somebody. It needs the force of the UN. It is imperative and not just an obligation for the US, because it is a weed that threatens the whole of humanity.

Many step beyond any form of rationalism. Their terror is not just a simple game between good and bad children, as many think while observing them on the city streets.

They invoke the jihad. This means that every Muslim is obliged to kill men who are different to them, as much in their own neighborhoods as anywhere else.

I think it is time that the West starts to treat the practice of Islam outside of the Islamic world like the Islamic world treats Christianity in its own states. On the other hand, they need to redefine their teachings about the Holy War. Many misuse it.

However, for the moment, it is an illusion, so there is only the American way to protect humanity. My words are not an exaggeration—I try to express the fear of many, and I just read the facts around me.

Somebody may get the impression that I hate someone. On the contrary, I do not have any reason to detest anybody, but I always have a reason to love. A Christian always needs to bless everybody, even enemies.

All the Holy Scriptures of all the religions intend to be noble books, but many who follow them are far removed from them. To kill anybody just because of a different faith is undoubtedly out of the question.

I have no pretensions to say anything in the name of any European, but I would like to tell many of them to shut up. I know many would like to tell me I speak for them. Our divisions are our wars.

Many want to stop the war, and I would like that too. Tolerance needs to be a universal trait of every personality, especially politicians, but a ceasefire needs to be in the greater interest.

Hundreds of millions of dogmatic insanities need to be pacified by healthy minds. The UN have to open their eyes and notice the wrong movements around us. To create an impact on everyday life, they need to be more responsible for what happens in the world, particularly the ever-growing extremism.

The paradox of our current time is how raw liberalism became the first dogmatic force in the world. They make unnatural acts, abortion, euthanasia, cloning, and other crazy things become our principal nature.

It creates the satanic religion of democracy or just a permanent time of carnival. Islamic fanaticism is also a response to our mistakes.

At the culmination of its death, each civilization was in a state of general immoral behavior (law). Therefore, it is evident, today more than ever, that many prepare for the apocalyptic time together with the jihadists. They are two parts of the same whole.

The Iraqis are victims of their dictator and at the same time "martyrs" of religious misuse. Can they be free from both evils? America brings the freedom of their country to them, but I do not believe the US will cure their spirits or misconceptions.

Terrorists need the liberation of the soul like they need bread and water. I am not sure anybody can help them. It is God's job. Sometimes a war is His way. Therefore, somebody has to be capable of isolating the extremists.

I did not mention Guantanamo, but I could suggest many Guantanamos for the many different extremists. However, there also needs to exist a place for those who violate nature and conscience in producing these terrorists. The terrorizing of traditional morals is a root of all others deviations around us.

We need to classify terrorism in accordance with nature and human rights. Different kinds of mob behavior (orchestrated by politicians, the media, religious leaders, etc.) produce terrorists, so these are the basic branches of terrorism.

I point out Amnesty International as well. I would like to be clear. I do not wish to limit anyone's human rights. Although many do not deserve the treatment they get in accordance with democratic values, it is a way to respect ourselves in spite of them and in spite of us.

Extreme liberalism is no different from anarchy, so we should have a law that puts the extreme liberals in order as well. However, the tragedy is that they make the laws. It will trigger holy war all around the world, because they are no different from jihadists.

The holy war will start soon in Europe, but it is not a battle against jihadists. It will be a war to protect our moral, healthy nature and the virtue of our tradition and dignity. Civil wars will take root among Europeans. It is our apocalypse, and we need to try to prevent it.

Everyday activities are relegated to second place. The war is a dominating theme, not just for the media but also for everybody. Some newspapers become a topic for themselves.

I am not American, and my power is not in any firearm, but I can turn off the TV.

The war starts to form my way of thinking. I understand that we all need America.

In my building, some people do some wrong things, and I say to them to change their behavior, or they will need the marines to put them in order.

Morals fall down on the scale of understanding, and many manic manners take the advantage over intellect. It is the right interpretation of the demonstrations. In a panic attack of the modern times, it is too late to speak about morals. I am afraid I am out of date.

If this is so, it is the end of Homo sapiens.

I like to say democracy, but it is not moral anymore, as we can see every day. For me, honesty needs to be the seed of democracy. Morals are the only medicines able to heal politicians, but they are clearly no longer in stock.

Morals do not mean religion. My religion is Life, and Life is moral. A moral needs to be life.

Some reports say the Iraqis have an order to use their chemical weapons against the Kurds. This is nothing new, especially not for the Kurds.

Gasmasks could soon be kept in pockets instead of handkerchiefs, but this will not help us find an answer to the madness of our times. A gasmask is just a temporary solution. The sense of life is more than a pocket game.

There is a new diplomatic standoff between Russia and the US because of Russian projectiles being used by the Iraqi army. Moscow refutes all the accusations and returns the ball, asking for an urgent session of the

UN Security Council to consider the war in Iraq. We have already seen it.

The attack on Baghdad systematically lasts a whole day. American tanks are 80 km away, near to the Iraqi capital.

I remember Vukovar and Sarajevo... Many think about Stalingrad. One day, somebody could be thinking the same about Baghdad.

Basra continues to resist.

Every 40 seconds, a person is killed in the world. This is the average for the last year. To give the data for this year would need help from the heavens.

Bush has declared, "The war is just starting."

Immaculate Conception

3/25/2003

President Bush demands an additional $75 billion from Congress.

The price of the war seems too high, even for Americans. Many protest that the country is unable to afford it. If they capitulate and give up the American principles, however, it would also give up their way of life. It would be to surrender the Christian civilization and lead to a liberal chaos and a paradise for the jihadists.

The UN needs to be responsible for war costs. Our democracy is blind. Bush tries to open the eyes of many Europeans, but I am afraid that only the power of God is able to do that.

Iraq refuses the humanitarian aid offered by the US and Britain, allegedly because of the price that would be paid for it.

The country's national pride (i.e., Saddam's pride) has an advantage with him being a dictator. He personally does not need the food and supplies, because he enjoys an abundance of everything.

It seems his government does not have any pretense anymore about caring about its citizens. However, after ten years of confrontation with the West, Iraq has lost any sense of reality. The extremism is a mistake of the UN too.

Today is the feast of the Immaculate Conception. One woman conceived by the word of an Angel, and Jesus Christ himself came later to save us. Mary from Nazareth became His Mother. This fact, I believe, speaks about another human dimension that is hidden from our eyes.

Some Christians do not accept the dogma of the Immaculate Conception, but surprisingly, Islam does take it seriously. It is a great thing among us, but nobody knows how to connect the chain of understanding. We need the Second Coming of the Son of God to put us in order.

The Koran says, like it does in the Bible, that Jesus will come again, but it also teaches that he will be Muslim and the leader of the Jihad. I don't believe He will be a Christian either—He will just be God.

It is too bad that people always point out differences to better their images. Selfishness is the reason why it seems that an unbridgeable abyss exists between religions.

The Pentagon repeats that Iraq is gradually losing control over land. Saddam refutes this and says that the after the enemy is trapped, it will be buried.

I remember Croatia. My little homeland obtained its liberty alone, but 25,000 Croats went to the City of God in the process.

It seems that some nations, like Iraq, are not capable of liberating themselves, because they are not ready to pay the price. Maybe they still do not deserve liberty!

I'm not sure it is always an appreciated role for America. Many need to thank the White House, especially Germany and France.

I understand if students demonstrate, and their reasons are unimportant. However, when teachers persuade their elementary school pupils to protest against the war, it is morally unacceptable for any purpose. Today is the feast of innocents, but I am not sure if any of them know it.

I am afraid that the behavior of some Europeans is an "immaculate" conception of the evil they will soon experience.

They seem to find the misuse of young souls easier than putting their minds to work and finding other solutions.

Everybody understands, because everyone was a child at some point, that children are not experts in the making of political messages. There are experts of manipulation, but they are not among the pupils.

Schoolchildren are always ready to leave the classroom, particularly if their teachers ask them to. It seems that disciplinarians sometimes like to play hooky as well.

All over the world, many people abuse children, not just educators but also those with different interests. In some countries, they are used as sacrificial soldiers.

Today, Europe propagates its pathological images. They insist on creating a European Army as soon as possible. Maybe they would also like to see teenagers with guns. Someone needs to prepare them, or maybe somebody has already done so.

Maybe it seems like democratic progress to provoke revolution with minors, or maybe some teachers continue to promote habits from their homelands.

In our own name, we must keep children far away from our misunderstandings. They are the last virtue of each civilization after the prostitution of the elders. Stop the misuse of children in whatever case! Let them just grow up.

The war culminates in battles for the bridges of Nassyria. The news speaks about new American bridgeheads.

Each bridge is a poem. Each one is an enigma for warriors. It is so easy to say many words about them. Each battle testifies that it is difficult to build a bridge over our mistakes. Death is the bridges' guardian. This is always so during wartime. It is a time of the shift of life.

Tensions increase between Turkey and the Kurds. The Turkish Army lurks ready to cross over the Iraqi border. Only some weeks before, their parliament refused to take part in the war. They shed their skins again, but will they ever change their nature? They try to prevent a Kurdish uprising in Turkey.

It is clear that America seriously intends to capture Baghdad as soon as possible. It seems that many citizens of the Iraqi capital support the invasion.

Some political leaders ask Saddam to leave Iraq. This would save many lives and prevent the destruction of the country, but his treasure is there, so his heart must be there as well, so he stays there.

Old Babylon trembles together with other archeological areas. Tanks destroy the hearts of dead civilizations to put Iraq in order. Some reports from Iraq blame the US.

I think about Babylon's mysteries and its biblical confusion of languages. Many people act like they come from that time, or maybe I just enjoy challenging some media.

In any case, nobody can satisfy the feast of the Immaculate Conception.

Sandstorm

3/26/2003

Basra shows its thousand faces.

The regular units are out of any control, and paramilitary forces terrorize the local inhabitants. Criminals accuse the Coalition of crimes they have done themselves. Is this a quality of holy warriors?

The media misuse every American rocket that fails to hit its target. Some experts try to blame the US, but lies blame many people.

One misguided bomb killed 15 people. Everybody knows that the Baghdad market was not a military target, especially not for the Americans. Reverence to innocent victims, however, collateral damage is unavoidable in any war.

Objective information loses its authority.

TV Al Jazeera has a monopoly on the information from Baghdad. It goes hand in hand with Saddam. It is a cosmetic mirror for Muslims worldwide, and many in the West take it seriously.

TV therapy creates and multiplies pockets of resistance in many cities. It tries to cure the Iraqi hearts that are lost in fear and encourage them to resist. Extremists travel there to help their brothers.

Propaganda will not help the Iraqis much. However, how many new victims will this kind of journalism cause in vain?

Al Jazeera is like a lighthouse for the Mujahedin, but the same can be said for the extreme-left Europeans. The anti-American campaign needs just this type of information, so they can use it to form public opinion.

I would like to say something about Sigmund Freud, but it is almost crazy to speak to some people about a Jew.

I catch fire in the presence of God's justice. I feel that all who do bad things will finish in the pit of their mistakes one day. The triumph of light will come. In spite of everything, it is our fate.

It is so because of the Mercy of God. It is hope for the future. The conversion toward the Lord is the last means of salvation, as much for many politicians as for sinners and criminals. Let's trust in Jesus!

There is logic behind why some officials think like they do. It's easy to find the key reason for their thoughts, because their moral compass is their image.

However, why do many journalists stray from their professional code into unacceptable behavior? I do not understand this. It's evident that some are jihadists with open eyes, while others look through eyeglasses of anti-Americanism, but both are blind to the world around them.

Evidently, those who form an everyday image of the war become the slaves of misunderstanding or the masters of propaganda. Nevertheless, for some, their job is to discredit the Americans.

In this time of terrorism and antiterrorism, there can be no oasis for lies anymore, not even in the Iraqi desert. It is time to chain up that beast.

The Pentagon is clearer than many other sources of information.

To be under the stars of the US flag is about more than the path of military success. In the shadow of its colors, I understand the truth better than on the other sides. The future depends on American courage. However, we also need to be there to lend moral support to the fight against terrorism.

I see the American banner as a holy symbol of antiterrorism. It resists the rites of burning committed by the newly combined hordes of anti-Americans worldwide that imitate their strayed brothers. It is the power of leadership to stop the terror.

Evil clones its children.

Every day, I put the media to the test, whether it be TV, radio (which I prefer), or newspapers that I read. I browse in the various languages I speak.

La Dernier Heure (A Belgian French-language daily) - *"Americans Deceive Security Council and Public Opinion" - "Forgeries Accuse Iraqis of Creating Atom Bomb"- "All Bush's Lies" -Etc...* (Free translation)

Guardian - I find there an outline of the reality. It seems that the war will not last forever, as some wish or just suppose. Classical newspapers seem like latecomers compared with the electronic media, so I gradually lose interest in spending a lot of time reading them.

In addition, even where there are governments who act favorably toward the US, anti-Americanism propagates its utopia.

The English Prime Minister, Tony Blair, goes to Washington.

Sandstorms begin hindering the Coalition troops.

Sometimes it seems that fate is more than a consequence of the past, because some people understand it better when they read it from their palms. They vigorously imagine things, so they will see what they wish to see, just as I think about some women.

They say that the game of destiny bound Bush to Iraq. For them, the bad weather is the time of the wrath of God.

I enjoy my metaphors again. Twelve years after the first Gulf War, a stormy voice resounds through the wind and writes with grains of sand the new message of the Iraqi desert: "My time comes again; A Bush comes again."

The storm puts America on the trails.

The Mujahedin prepare the Islamic revolution in Basra. The resistance of the jihadists ensures that Basra suffers more than anybody can bear. They do not respect life, nor do they appreciate the 10,000 years of history and culture of this ancient city. Basra follows the path of its "martyrs" against the will of the majority of its inhabitants.

The need for food and water radically changes people. Bad men become worse, and the worst people become even worse. Basra becomes a prison for the population and a home for fanatics. Because of the battle, humanitarian access is blocked. In spite of its resistance, it is clear that the city must accept the will of the British.

Civilians are both the victims and the means for the Holy War. The population of Basra is ashamed. Strangers lead them against strangers. They do not have the opportunity to make a choice.

Today, I have new neighbors, two girls. This time Islam comes to my door with beauty at first sight. I am afraid that I only see the surface. I feel there are fears among us, in spite of our good will. I long for better days.

In fear, a nice thing can be so far from us, even when it is on our doorstep. Tolerance is a gift from heaven, but it is not easy to exercise its virtue.

I try to be patient toward my patience.

If you do not believe in fate, it does not mean you can escape it. I just feel nostalgic at the moment.

I do not like to be a surrogate anywhere, so I try to enjoy my country wherever I am. It means being as far away from oneself as you are from reality.

When I look at refugees who run away from their roots, I force myself to think about the sense of life. It needs to show any evil master that we can enjoy the paradise in our homes only if we are free. However, it is a way of suffering.

It is clear that the famous biblical fig leaf is the only treasure many bring with them. Migrants always have a nostalgic image of their homelands.

Adam and Eve were the first misplaced persons. I am afraid that fate dreams in our genes, even if we change them.

Maybe, my soul speaks too much about nostalgia, because it needs to return to the lost paradise of its homeland.

First, I would like to stop the war and cease the battles everywhere, right at this moment. I love peace, but I know it is not possible without sacrifices. Therefore, all the prophets will be revealed in the name of peace.

I know many men dream what I dream, but in spite of this, we are as different as night and day. I comprehend many countries and their governments as a homeland for terrorism, and they try to spread it anywhere they can.

The media reappearance of Saddam conveys his message to Muslims again: to fight the Jihad. Only a repetition of it is as horrible as his words. He points out the victory will be in the name of God.

I do not really know how to write out the many names of God in English, nor do I want to learn. For me, the name of God is sacred. Jehovah is my God.

I cannot accept any other name, although I respect them all. However, I believe there is only one God. He is misused by many, believers as much as atheists. God belongs to everybody, so respect should be required of everyone.

Many extremists catch a suicidal infection, manifesting their wrath in response to Saddam's superstition. I am afraid there is no gate of light for fanaticism. Each moment, the fanatics sink deeper into their abyss.

The USA can be the whip or the gift of rationalism for many, but it depends on their choices. In the hard Islamic heads, America is literally the great Satan, so no good thing can come from there. The virus of misunderstanding eats all logic.

I hold no illusions that anybody needs to persuade other people to change religion. Everybody needs to respect each other's religions, but can some people reconsider their behaviors (beliefs) before they die as suicidal meat? I see them as children of terrorism. Islam itself is not responsible for them straying toward terrorism.

Iraq continues to exaggerate the Coalition's losses while hiding the death toll of its own soldiers. It is such bad propaganda that it cannot be taken seriously by any rational mind.

It seems again that the Turks have crossed over the Iraqi border. They go in and out from time to time. Many believe that there is no humane element in their treatment of the Kurds, and this accords with their Ottoman tradition. Their new government stares into the future through the colors of Islam. Are the Europeans in danger because of them?

Turkey becoming a part of Europe is a very important step in the plans of the Mujahedin. It means that all land conquered from Islam over the course of history needs to be returned within the borders of the so-called universal Islamic state. They will fight for it, but no rational mind will allow it. I do not hate anybody, but I love Europe.

The war could create more complications. The Turks detest the Kurds. They also do not love Iraq, nor do they appreciate the US. They are afraid of America, so they will continue to maintain an image of friendship.

I am worried again that the Kurds will once more become victims of their fate to be a condemned nation forever. The American operations could be justified just by bringing freedom to these poor people.

The Americans deny their weapons are missing targets as often as some claim.

President Bush gave a speech in Florida. He points out that 48 nations support the US and the war. The Coalition is leading Iraq toward freedom. The public understands him, and this gives an impression that America is not divided.

"May God bless America and its allies, this time like always," said Bush.

Bush attracts good spirits with the spirit of his Christianity and his character. Evil cannot love him or any other noble person. For many, him and his country are the last hope of the moral humanity. Without him, America will touch the chaos of civilizations, together with others.

According to some researchers of the Holy Scripture, the American helicopters and fighter jets are similar to apocalyptic images of "grasshoppers" in the New Testament, and the tanks are like "fire monsters."

This time, Turkey represents the moon under the feet of the apocalyptic woman, with the crown of 12 stars around her head being a metaphor for the EU flag. She is a virgin clothed in the sun, which is the symbol of Christianity and God who is Christ (Rev.12).

If this really is the meaning of the prophecy, and if we are at the threshold of Armageddon, then we have no choice other than to take our side in the Holy War. To be or not to be is a damned question this time. We cannot avoid the future.

I am not a crusader, nor do I believe any American is, but the conditions urge us to be ready to defend our roots and our lives. Can Europe understand that it does not have a future in persecuting Christianity and its dreams?

Of course, it is not a job for agnostics. Liberals have strayed to see their side lost in a wood of their permanent nights. They prepare the Apocalypse, so they need the jihadists. I'm just not sure they are aware of it.

Terrorism and its devils create a Hell on Earth. Of course, there is a difference between terrorists and demons, but we need to take the former more seriously than the latter. Some people think that demons do not exist, but this does not mean that terrorists do not live among us.

This is my response to those who accuse America of crusading against jihadists: If it is like that, they asked for it.

About 1,000 Iraqis have lost their lives in the last three days.

Under the cover of a sandstorm, Iraq tries to use an opportunity to take the initiative over the Coalition troops. They conduct a massive movement toward the outskirts of the cities. They suppose it is a good time to move their tanks because the weather is not favorable for the American air force.

Visibility is so bad they can literally see a finger in front of their noses. An analyst predicts chaos of never-seen-before dimensions. The anti-American voices of the Arab media speak about the weather as a trap delivered by God for the Coalition.

Some speculate that it is time for the Iraqi special units to cause some diversions. Others believe that Iraq is incapable of realizing such tasks because the Iraqis are still slaves to the traditional static tactics of the Soviets.

Reports speak about 700 tanks forming a ring around Baghdad. The south of the city holds their main concentration. The marines are there. The same news comes from Basra.

I don't know what to think about all I have heard. I'm not sure the Iraqis have resolved to commit suicide, nor do I think they want to become martyrs, not yet. However, I know that the Americans fly, even if the birds do not, and they can see through darkness better than any bird.

American parachute units land in the north of Iraq and join with the Kurds to open a new front.

I hear the swan song of the Iraqis. The sandstorm will not save them.

Anti-American Newspaper

3/27/2003

It is morning, and doves flutter up in front of my window. I need the power of the Holy Spirit to understand the cacophony from the media.

Even now, when the generals thought that the situation was under control, the battles are renewed.

Paratroopers in the north of Iraq draw the biggest attention at this moment.

The Shiites and Sunnites, normally poles apart, make an anti-American union. Among them exists a difference, but they die for Islam first and for Saddam second.

The Kurds also live their own form of schizophrenia. One part collaborates with the regime, while the others work with the Americans.

I am saturated with the permanent repetition of news and confused by all the contradictory information. My thoughts start to resist the media's occupation.

A week of war is a hard thing to follow unconditionally. I want to put my little things of everyday life first.

Some opinions point out the conflict between civilizations that started on 9/11/2001. Some people see things that others either do not notice or have no interest in. The war provokes many questions.

The SARS issue is easily compared with an apocalyptic illness. However, I hope it is not that time yet.

The time will come when people will ask to die, but they will not find death. The living will be jealous of the dead, as says the Apocalypse.

Islamic demonstrations call for other Muslims to fight the Jihad. The war is a gift to them. They enjoy striking at the US.

Arabs shout, "Kill Bush!" The Europeans play a similar melody by screaming, "Bush is a killer." The only difference between them is their choice of words.

The world is too divided. It seems there is no hope for any of us, except for those who believe in life after death.

Tony Blair tries to secure a bigger role for the UN. There is an opinion that America would lose its self-control without him.

He is like a dove among hawks that manages to keep its feathers. However, he knows that without the hawks, it would not be possible to realize any peace.

No, I do not believe that he is really a dove, nor do I think that Bush is a hawk. The question is not so simple. The world has become too vulgar to respect it with good manners. Therefore, from time to time, the hawks need to become doves and the doves need to become hawks to put it in order.

The Iraqi reaction to his words is again a cliché of humoristic nonsense: "Blair is a little whiter than Bush, so he has comprehended that Iraq will never accept the authority of strangers."

On the Arab side, the extreme hate toward America expresses its face like their animosity toward Israel. I am afraid that nobody could easily correct the irrationality among them.

Brussels is a jungle of cement, literally and figuratively. One can meet this impression with every step. However, I do like the capital of Europe. It is a more agreeable city than many I know. Walking is always an inviting prospect.

I try to catch a breath of silence by changing my environment to protect myself from the media bombardment.

It is not possible to be alone anywhere, because you have a feeling that something is wrong wherever you go. Police cameras survey us, and electronic eyes are the biggest monster of our time. However, I understand the need for them.

Brussels is under severe control, and this is mainly good. However, human nature has a need to experience the primordial beauty of untouched things.

The Iraqis hurry to the peripheries of their cities to move their tanks out of their desperate positions. While I think about one peaceful corner, I consider this: Is it impossible to avoid the war, or do I just not know how?

I feel that all I love needs more projection in the heart of my yearnings. I am afraid that I'm just a part of the general mess around me.

I finally end up in the library. I browse some Belgian newspapers, but I cannot find any original news.

I find there is a great disdain for anything that comes from America, except for the odd article from American newspapers that helps to support their attitudes.

I do not believe this is a general image of Belgium, because I know many people think differently.

French journalists promote opinions that are diametrically opposed to a healthy mind. They point out the American mistakes and openly support the Iraqi resistance.

I like different colors when painting, but this time I have no intentions of organizing an exhibition of ignorance. Nevertheless, I express a black-and-white impression that I understood from the newspaper lines.

No one can objectively describe journalism these days, but I think the main British papers (*The Guardian*, *The Times*, etc.) keep a traditional sense for true information.

The Italian *La Republic* observes everything through its emotive but respectful style.

From its diagrams, I have a good understanding of the disposition of the troops. For an instant, I stop before the front line around Baghdad. It is a feeling of reality I cannot find everywhere.

Afterwards, I have the impression that I've done something wrong. Many things are not clear at all, or maybe I need more time to put my thoughts in order. I fear that no progress is possible with the outlines I found there.

I finish up with the Belgian Dutch-language newspapers. I am sure there are two voices in Belgium.

Anti-Americanism is the barbarism of modern time. Atheists and holy warriors walk together to hell. It is a time of black-and-white Mujahedin all around us.

I fight against the media addiction.

The British soldiers create a cemetery of Iraqi tanks around Basra, much like how Croatian forces created the same thing around Vukovar from Serbian armor.

The Sandstorm has gone, and the situation has become more realistic. It is clear that fortune will not be an important factor, because it always follows those with courage rather than those who calculate.

If America needs years to win the victory, it means we leave the time of lost generations. Terror changes our habits. We all need conversion to find the way for the salvation of the world.

At first sight, it is absurd, but we have to accept that some men enjoy dying while killing others.

The permanent sticking points among the irrational possibilities are Arab solidarity with the greater Islamic world, the reawakening of the lost

Russian pride, China's fear of the coming of democracy, and the atomic adventures of some countries.

I trust in the Divine Mercy.

I see America as the only rational power and the only superpower in the service of humanity.

Mines in the bay of Basra invoke a spirit of Princess Diana.

TV Al Jazeera compares itself to CNN. It persists in the distorted reality of the Arab world. It is a mine of illusions. Maybe it believes that it really gives objective news.

It defines itself by its calumnies. Most of Islam's networks are portrayed in subjective comments and images by the media.

It shows its face to those who enjoy it, so they can enjoy it more. It is a misuse of journalism. Its spectators enjoy its facade more than any true information.

Al Jazeera understands what Muslims like to watch better than others do. Therefore, it offers them a product they love. This is the reason why America lost the media war among Muslims.

Americans continue to realize the victory for those who will accept it. It is a tragedy that many do not want to understand anything outside of Islam.

I am afraid that Iraq will need a permanent protection force, like Kosovo. Who will provide it and pay for it? The UN is below the level of responsibility needed for the time being.

Europe lights up its sides more and more. However, the divisions are clear. Many do not wish to pay the American war costs, like they did after the first Gulf war.

I would understand better if they were capable of taking the role of America by any means.

A surprising declaration by the French government says they will enter the war if Iraq uses WMDs, but it is only a sign of cynicism.

Bush is not an appropriate political leader for the shape of the European antichrist's new world order. Some therefore fire up the situation to escape more easily from their moral obligations.

I am afraid for the future of the EU. I feel Britain would rather become a new American state than a coherent part of an EU under French and/or German domination.

Fears buzz around us. If the war would pass beyond the Iraqi borders, nobody could stay out, not even Germany. Hypothetical questions are too serious.

It is a double ring around Baghdad. Both sides prepare their tanks, and some think it will be one of the biggest tank battles in history.

Iraqis again evoke the memory of Stalingrad and the Second World War. It seems they need the smell of brave souls from that time. They push the burden of fears to America. They try to inject the image of fascism into the Coalition.

The Americans destroyed the Iraqi TV station. Iraqis do not have the right to a satellite link.

In the morning, it seems like some news is coming from people who are still asleep. However, in the evening, it gives the impression that some journalists go to bed too early. I am not always sure it is because of time-zone differences.

Although I try to catch up with the all-important news, I am not sure that I am always up to date. I hope that I am not out of date if I say that humanitarian aid reaches the land.

This time, I am sure it's time to go to sleep and forget the burden of the media and its anti-Americanism.

To Be in Fashion

3/28/2003

According to the first news this morning, the night has passed without any new nightmares.

All the commentaries just sound like the repetition of old stories.

The Iraqi press representative tries to keep a level of conviction, maintaining his hope in lies. "We are winning, and we will be the winner," he said.

I browse a daily newspaper, *The Times*, and read a feature about the *Orange Yellow Desert*. That sandstorm really was like hell.

The explosions, the bombardment, the rockets, the killing, the persecution, and so on are an inevitable price of freedom.

I learn to be patient with the media. Although I am never satisfied with journalism, I enjoy information. It bombards contradictions at any one time, but I persist nonetheless. The more I try to respect it, the more it offends me.

I keep my rhythm. I learn how to select news from the media. Sometimes, just knowing the stance of some people is enough to determine whether to reject or accept their reports.

On average, six or seven Coalition soldiers die each day. On the Iraqi side, you would need to multiply that number by at least five.

I try to estimate the civilian casualties, but this is impossible because of unreliable data. In any case, it no doubt surpasses the military casualties.

Le Monde, a French daily paper, makes a joke about America. It seems to be in accordance with the popularity of President Chirac, who feigns a smile for the Nobel Prize.

Channels filled with crude oil spark the imagination of many analysts.

I moved from my armchair and tried in vain to correct some strange sounds coming from my radio. Disappointed, I looked at the portrait on the wall, as I do many times every day, because it is a picture of the woman I love. This time, however, I noticed a ring I thought I had lost a long time ago. It was fixed over the frame.

In that moment, I realized how it is possible to be blind, despite your eyes, when you see only what you want to see. I understood that some commentators perceive only what they can consciously see at first sight. Using this logic, I understand the speculation about the rings around Baghdad.

I believe the Americans are capable of finding solutions to all the Iraqi traps, and they will not need months, like I did to find my ring.

Fifty civilians died in Baghdad.

An Imam, a kind of Islamic cleric, marches with a gun among the fanatics and calls for the jihadists to resist. The Pentagon did not deny the massacre.

America prepares 100,000 new soldiers. Many Muslims think that Iran will be the next target.

In Basra, the Iraqis hold out white flags in their masses. It seems to have come into fashion!

Some "modern" opinions among the Arabs claim that America's generals have an interest in the killing of civilians.

I do not wish to be in fashion, so I have no comment.

Demonstrations

3/29/2003

I listen to dirges all over Baghdad. The death of innocent civilians touches even the most zealous supporters of the war. Although there has never been a war without collateral damage to civilian areas, this cannot be much consolation for the victims.

Syria and Iran threaten to enter the war if America violates their territory again.

The demonstrations reach their culmination, and something urges me to think about those useless creatures again. I would like to suggest they reorganize themselves and make the march to Baghdad.

We all need to use more of Gandhi's methods.

Millions of pacifists on a mission of goodwill could be more effective than any military force. It could be a wise investment for someone who would lose money because of the war.

However, I am not convinced that among this worldwide multitude there really exists a majority ready to do anything for peace. Their parades just provide unwise support for terrorism.

For a long time already, the noise before the American embassy in Brussels spreads loud messages in vain. The youths make a joke in the name of peace, but they are too naive.

Many among them use the opportunity to manifest their jihadist ideas. One group of strange people in front of camera imagines they are in a mosque.

One newspaper calls on citizens to boycott Coca-Cola products and McDonald's restaurants, and TV reports confirm the realization of this idea. Some people do it with great passion, but I see it as an angry fly on the tail of an elephant.

The terrestrial globe becomes more divided by day and night; this time, it is just the black-and-white division of minds.

More and more nations support the US. Civilization is like a fragile curtain.

I do not believe the Europeans have fallen back to the level of the Second World War, but it is shameful that Europe is such a nest of anti-Semitism. It is a major reason for the European anti-Americanism.

Many have forgotten they enjoy their freedom thanks to the sacrifice of many Americans.

Kill the Americans and any who refuse to fight them is the motto of the Iraqi jihadists gathered from all over the world.

A comment posed a question about the logic of soldiers dying in the 21st century.

The BBC tries to heal wounded consciences and fearful hearts with extravagant sporting events. Today is the soccer match between Croatia and Belgium. I'm ready to follow it.

I remember the jihadists in Bosnia and Herzegovina. I think about their influence on the Islamic population there and its awful consequences for the future, not just for the Balkans.

Time produces the children of fanaticism like mushrooms after the rain. After the moral dimension, this is the main reason why I prefer the American side.

I go out to feel the soul of the city again. I am disappointed. It seems that drops of rain leave their clouds to follow me. Today, an umbrella is the next thing after the Jihad that I dislike.

I notice a Belgian woman near me with the hat of a Belgian soccer fan, like the crown on the head of the Statue of Liberty in New York.

The city center is very busy. Rivers of people after the everyday demonstrations are there like furious termites. Its iconography eats the sense of life and healthy minds.

Fanatics from Syria pass over the Iraqi border. These groups of volunteers are already dead in the depths of their damnation.

The British deny the four-day plan for the occupation of Baghdad. Four American soldiers are the victims of a car bomb.

I enjoy the news from Croatia. It sometimes gives me more than other European sources, or maybe I understand it better.

There was an earthquake. Its epicenter was at Croatia's furthest island of the Adriatic, "Jabuka" (meaning "Apple"). Nature moves my imagination. For me, and for this time, it is a symbolic name. I remember the twin towers in New York. Heaven wants to point out the true reason for the Iraq war.

It gives me the wings to fly to my gardens. I feel that an apple escaped from paradise again and trembled in my heart. I love my Eden. It is my Croatia.

I know I exaggerate, but if I do so, it's because I want to make something more understandable. The war in Iraq creates sweet metaphors this time.

The Apocalypse predicts earthquakes and volcanic eruptions as signs of the greatest catastrophes. The firestones, which will fall from the clouds, are compared by some with the bombs and missiles.

Fifty-six people have died of the SARS virus. The Italian doctor who first encountered the virus in Vietnam already enjoys the other side of life.

The disorder of the universe is the next step of our end.

The Iraqi government, with the help of some western lawyers, asks for permission to try President Bush for war crimes.

Pope John Paul II warns, through his charismatic words, that the war provokes new divisions among religions. I think nobody better can create a bridge for it before Jesus himself comes again.

Finally, Iraqi soldiers have aimed at the Kuwait capital. By chance, there are no civilian victims.

Anti-Americans continue to blame the Americans.

Masks

3/30/2003

Many Iraqis are forced by the terror of the Mujahedin to sacrifice their lives against their will. God is a misused figure.

Two hospitals are closed in Ontario because of SARS. I am afraid I will not be travelling soon.

The citizens of Hong Kong wear masks against the virus. It goes far, too far. The fear of SARS creates a new carnival rite.

There is new bombing chaos again. I understand the everyday suffering of people. I look at the images of my heart and the real-life stories from my homeland.

American bombs try to make an educated choice, while the Serbs preferred to target civilians, so the Iraqis are relatively happy.

Baghdad is in the trap. The threat of WMDs creates fear among the coalition troops, because the Iraqi beast is dying. It could be the last gambit of the Iraqi regime.

It is Sunday morning, a time to go to church. I stay at home, however. I am like someone who tries to show solidarity with the Iraqi Christians. I watch a TV mass.

One priest reports from Baghdad. He is a prisoner of circumstances, but his voice spreads hope. He is out of the media trend.

Four thousand Mujahedin have crossed the Iraqi border. According to American intelligence sources, this is just pure propaganda. However, if it were true, it would be worse than a WMD attack.

The Apaches have made a suicidal mistake again because of technical failure.

Rumsfeld says in a speech that the British troops at Basra should be proud. He is the Secretary of Defense, and Bush's strong hand is not always under control.

The UN mission in Kabul has been bombed. The American Army is stretched out like Jesus on the Cross.

There is anxiety that elements from al-Qaeda are searching for Iraq's WMDs. Maybe they just need a mirror.

It is obvious the Iraqi leader is becoming nervous. Channels filled with crude oil are blazing around Baghdad.

Some Islamic theologians point to the clash of civilizations. This justifies the jihadists. According to them, Islam is being humiliated worldwide. Chechnya, Afghanistan, Bosnia and Herzegovina, Palestine, Iraq, and so on serve as their examples.

It seems like Saddam is a cat with nine lives. He is again under a degree of speculation. Some are afraid for his life, while others wish for his disappearance as soon as possible, but many are curious.

The European Union tries to express a unified political voice in response to the US, but it is just a cock-and-bull story. Many Europeans do not realize they are part of it. It is just a union of interests and occasional love.

It is the first shift of the American soldiers.

"No blood for oil" is the message of some demonstrators in Boston. Some Americans are like many Europeans, and some Europeans are like many Arabs.

There is a flood of inscriptions through the streets of Brussels: *"Not in my name."*

A suicide-bomber attack has destroyed the Cafe London in Netanya, Israel. It is not just fanatically inspired but also intended as a symbolic response to the Iraqi Basra tale.

The Islamic countries show their towering rage with violent demonstrations. There is too much noise to understand anything, but everything is clear. These images produce suicide bombers as a gift for Iraq.

The Iraqi leadership invites its soldiers to bury the bodies of the enemy on the battlefield. They probably want to say to frightened Iraqis that Americans are dying as well.

A river of refugees has gushed up from Basra under the fire of Mujahedin. The jihadists dress up in civilian clothes to better mask themselves among the inhabitants. Baghdad denies the report despite losing control of Basra.

Some men use masks in vain.

Green Color

3/31/2003

Brussels is an anti-American montage of variously colored dilettantes. It is like a strange public book containing thousands of inscriptions in several languages and alphabets.

In the main street of the city center, I read on the wall of one building that Americans are the killers of children.

I take out my four-color pencil to cross it out. By chance, I do it with a green line. It is a color the jihadists adore. I hope that my green line tells them that their nonsense is not acceptable to everybody. Although I think like this, the best way to show your mind to such people is to stop speaking with them, just as Arthur Schopenhauer, one of the greatest European philosophers, wrote in his time.

Many misuse democratic rules and the abundance of freedom to offend others. The Islamism of Brussels is the great temptation for Belgian democracy.

Europe is very naive about the Islamic deviations. Their task is clear, to make Islam prevalent everywhere. The European left-wing monsters welcome the extremists as partners against Christianity. In the West, many churches became mosques, because for the liberal-anarchists, money is the only measure of virtue.

To implant Islam, they indoctrinate their understanding of religion by force or by martyrdom if it is not possible by preaching.

Some European countries will soon become Islamic paradises, and some are already there. Many European cities are literally creating colonies for them, while Bosnia and Herzegovina, Macedonia, Kosovo, Albania, Cyprus, Bulgaria, and Greece still suffer from the centuries of Islamic occupation. It is like the Balkans' first syndrome.

If you look at how Christians live in the Islamic world, you don't need to be a prophet to see the European future.

Terrorism will not spare Europe despite its anti-Americanism.

I see that chaos will provoke a Christian response to protect their values. It is only needed because the masters of the new world order are unnatural and immoral creatures. They are incapable of maintaining the balance of power in the world. Their ideology is secularity, but this will never be a reasonable solution for the people. They misuse America and the whole world.

Europe is also a tool the jihadists need to realize their aims against the US. The Holy War is a thing of planetary dimensions, while the politicians who rule in the world are, as a rule, just local players. Such a global movement does not have a great future.

Bush is different from that spirit of the world, so he is on the stake. He is simply a unique politician and a rare believer in a mainly agnostic environment.

If the would-be extremists possessed the power that America has, it would either be the end of life on Earth or the realization of the Islamic "paradise" for everyone, including their atheistic supporters. Is terrorism a consequence of their understanding and the beginning of general disorder, from which something new will be born?

The Earth has its only future in the conversion of humanity. It is a paradox, but the main reason for the discord between religions is the domination of liberal chaos, which violates moral human virtues, in the world. It could be a synonym for agnosticism and their way of creating the new world order. In that mission, atheists are their main servants.

Muslims see in it the children of the Bible, while Christians see it in the jihadist Muslims. Agnostics misuse democracy, while Mujahedin misuse the Jihad.

The liberal-anarchists are exclusively bad sprouts from the Christian roots. Christianity strayed through the traps of agnosticism, while Islam lost its orientation in fanaticism. I therefore say they go hand in hand as children of the Apocalypse. This is the main reason I am not a crusader, because I see the causes of the mess on both sides.

Moral Christianity is the hope for the salvation of civilization and the medicament that many will refuse, choosing to die rather than change the images of their hearts. Maybe it has to be like this. Regardless, He will come to judge everybody.

Can the West, in any way, suffer it anymore because many cannot suffer the West anymore? Why do the jihadists provoke their martyrdom?

They kill others and call them killers. It is narcissistic nonsense, and the philosophy of egoism consequently surpasses our understanding. The Jihad is the question: Islam or nothingness.

Europe will not comprehend before it is forced to fight for its survival at home. It could already be too late. Many liberals are so far from their roots that they would rather become Muslims than walk hand in hand with reality.

I say liberals, but I refer to all atheists with an agnostic mask far removed from the light, all those who deny the law of nature to humiliate God's commands, and all the wicked people. And these can be found everywhere.

Those who do not understand the truth very often stray in the search for it. Democracy is the sword of Damocles.

The Catholic Church, like any other religion, is no exception, because some believers are the only shame of Christianity, despite that institution being the moral cornerstone of the world.

Do we need to protect our civilization or just ourselves? Is it just a simple question of terrorism? Maybe the liberals would find the answer if they changed their mirrors.

Can America (the America of George W. Bush) help the world to open its third eye before it becomes the liberal apocalyptic prey of the relativism of all virtues? It is the first enigma of the salvation of the world.

This time, it is a question of existence and not just the discord of coexistence. We need to understand how to survive. I am not a Darwinist, but I believe he was more than just the atheist many think he was. I am afraid he lived in the wrong time. He could maybe better explain some natural things to us if he were alive now.

Not all liberals are antichrists. We need to keep our mind in the rhythm of everyday images, to notice the signs of our time and the future, and to make a difference between good and bad. The only rules without exceptions should be the Ten Commandments of God, and they should be the foundation of everyday life. Otherwise, democracy will not survive, and the world could fall into general secular slavery or the dictatorship of elites.

The Apocalypse will start soon, or it has already started if we accept the terror of the jihadists just as terrorism. Many governments do, because they are better informed than the masses. Opinions that point to extremism as a means to provoke the clash of civilizations, have some merit in that case and do not belong to the group of useless conspiracy theories.

Therefore, I say liberals support terrorism. I am not judging liberals but rather just giving my opinion.

I listen to some new nonsense from Iraq. The Iraqis are calling on Americans to surrender.

The Marines go straight to Baghdad in spite of very fierce street fighting in some regions.

The SARS virus takes victims like the wind takes dry leaves. It is the first case of pneumonia in Belgium.

The Americans have crossed over the red line, which Iraq designated as the last line of defense around the capital.

Some towns and holy places are surrendering without resistance.

The Iraqi government threatens that it will defend Baghdad with any means. It spreads the fear that they will use chemical weapons.

I always feel nervousness in my fingers before awful news, but I feel nothing this time, so I am not afraid.

Syria is supporting the Iraqi regime. Colin Powell (the US Secretary of State) declares that such states need to suffer the consequences of their behavior.

Journalists continue to pay for their wartime roles with their lives. Last year, 16 reporters were killed, which was actually the lowest number of the last ten years.

There are additional security measures at the American airports. Journey becomes an adventure.

I would like to make my green cross the news.

Babylon

4/01/2003

There is panic in Belgium because of the SARS virus.

In Iraq, some women and children have been shot at a checkpoint.

It seems that fear and weariness become the first American problems. Sometimes it is not easy to make the choice of whether to kill or risk being killed.

The media's blind campaign against America loses the breath of tolerance. Anti-Americanism becomes a global village divided only by time zones.

The Pentagon justifies its soldiers. The threat of suicide attacks spreads insecurity, and many are haunted.

The US are blamed even because of Britain. Anti-Americans, with their shapeless minds being popular with the public, do not respect anything out of their order. They are either jihadists or unwilling supporters of holy warriors.

Bush says that every day, America gets nearer to capturing Baghdad. He suffers numerous inputted stupidities, but he manifests the traits of one man. His force is in his army and his clear mind in public relations.

One Belgian artist exaggerates his caricatures on TV. He shows Americans as ridiculous prostitutes.

Scientists warn that floods and tsunamis could soon come because of a great disturbance in the universe. It seems to be citing the Apocalypse. We live on the eve of apocalyptic events.

The battle for Baghdad starts. There are opinions that the city will peacefully accept the strangers. The Americans say that the next few days will give a clearer image.

The white flag is a simple and powerful sign of salvation for 8,000 Iraqis.

In a room next to my apartment, there is a very strange atmosphere tonight. A woman invites spirits through ritual magic. Some men from an African tribe shout out like devils.

It seems that the woman speaks all of the African languages in her trance. It reminds me of the biblical confusion of languages, because her voice is like the noise of tanks in the Iraqi land of Babylon, just as I heard it on television.

A hijacked aircraft from Havana has landed in Florida accompanied by two American fighters. Planes become like Halloween toys.

I have learned from the media that the spread of the SARS virus occurs through touch and through the air. It is again a fragment from the Apocalypse.

Instead of Saddam, his Minister of Information reads a message to the Iraqis that all Muslims should support the Jihad.

Today, I have finished reading the fourth book of the Gospel. It always tells me something new, and it's always only the truth. I have an idea that Saint John knows more about the current situation than all the media put together.

I compare my dear book with the TV, which often reports something new, yet the media enjoys deceiving even when it speaks the truth. It is the time of deception.

Forty thousand Fedayeen dressed as civilians represent the main danger for the Coalition. The Fedayeen are fanatical paramilitaries that were established under the command of Saddam's son twenty years ago

They are known to hold up white flags as bait for suicide attacks. They are the most faithful children of Saddam's agony.

America conquers new cities.

The predictions of the anti-American media are crashing down like the Tower of Babel.

Doubts

4/02/2003

The past two weeks have survived in the traces of my pen.

The media does not change the colors of its comments. Although the images are different from at the beginning of the conflict, the media still dances to the same tune.

The Iraqi press representative declares that the enemy did not capture anything important.

Where is the truth here? Maybe his message is aimed at those who always believe him, so he therefore has no interest in reporting facts.

The Americans are 30 km from Baghdad. It is too near, or still too far, for some analysts, but it is just enough for the doubts among Iraqis to culminate.

Victory is coming. This is not just a phrase of President Bush—it also occurs to everyone who has not strayed into the anti-Coalition propaganda.

Someone not adept at decoding information would be unable to decide between the divided media. Some skeptics change their stance through cleaner personal eyeglasses.

The State Department and the Pentagon demonstrate different approaches to the postwar reconstruction of Iraq.

For me, it is just a game. America asks for a way to improve its image in the eyes of the UN. For a moment, the war in Iraq is shadowed by it. It may be a sensible process, but somebody needs to promote its political position.

Some sources accuse Rumsfeld of using the war for his personal interests. Some try to achieve their aims through doubts, but I do not understand their intentions. I do not believe in the stories of the war for crude oil.

Tony Blair again petitions the UN. It needs to gain more control over Iraq as soon as possible. He needs some peace at home.

There is a doubt that the American tactics have not been successful. For some, it is easy to be a general after the battles.

The Pentagon, without any signs of nervousness, asserts that everything is going according to plan.

A key bridge over the Tigris is now under American control.

Two divisions of the Iraqi Republican guard have been destroyed. The ring around Baghdad is broken.

I have no doubts.

It Is Art

4/03/2003

They are on the doorstep. The marines are only 10 km from Baghdad.

The Iraqis spare their bridges, and this helps the Americans to move faster than anybody thought possible. They cross the Tigris and Euphrates as if they were the Mississippi.

Al Jazeera has lost the battle for the Iraqi morality. The Americans might have lost the battle for Iraqi hearts, but it seems they are invincible.

Some journalists have left Baghdad.

Meanwhile extremists hide tanks in Mosques.

I am surprised. In the springtime, even bears wake up from their dreams, but many Europeans are in a special kind of hibernation. This generation is lost in dreams.

The news from Hong Kong gives some hope for the future. Some SARS patients have recovered.

I am worried. I have seen Asian faces on the Metro. The virus spreads fear, and some people keep their distance. They are afraid of catching the infection.

I am concerned when people suffer because of their ethnicity or skin color. It shows that our democracy is not ready to survive modern fears. Our instincts still rule us.

Iraq is lost in the labyrinth-like mind of its leaders. It has no chance of escaping without American help.

It is foolish to expect Saddam to surrender Baghdad and deliver himself to the enemy, although this would be the cleverest decision of his dictatorship.

Saddam has probably found another solution for himself. His citizens are just there on a suicide mission to protect him.

He could have ended his own life like Hitler. Suicide is a highlight for cowardice, but he is known for trying to be brave in vain. He does not have the character of a martyr, even if he produces them.

Secret negotiations become very interesting. The Pentagon denies speculation about a ceasefire. Only unquestionable capitulation is acceptable for that to happen.

Saddam is alive. He says, "Iraq has used only a third of its potential." It is clear that he needs more time to find a better shelter.

Colin Powell is in Brussels trying to recruit NATO for future peacekeeping forces.

The Marines take control of Nasiriya. We can see some of them in the role of humanitarian workers. America shows a human face to the Iraqis.

Drinking water is a key problem for the country.

It is the desperate behavior of the jihadists. Some Fedayeen catch up with artists in trying to imagine how they can lift the morale of the citizens.

The French and the US continue to wear different eyeglasses. A boycott of goods occurs on both sides.

Iraqi loudspeakers repeat that the enemy does not control any of the Iraqi capital city. It says, "They are merely moving everywhere like snakes in the desert."

Some people have wonderful imaginations. It is clear that the Fedayeen know this, so they try to use it through art. However, if this was the solution, it would have already been used a long time ago. There is no exit for fanatics.

There is a fierce battle for Baghdad's airport. The Iraqi capital spends its nights in darkness.

Art is not the solution for Iraq, but the solution could be in art.

Secret Weapons

4/04/2003

The Americans control Baghdad International Airport, although Al Jazeera reports that the battle continues. It tries to postpone the bad news.

Some French journalists think that America has an obligation to renew the lost Iraqi paradise, even while the fighting continues.

A group of American Indians, refugees from South America, sells souvenirs in the center of Brussels. It is an opportunity that people receive from the other America.

They are not just an exotic light in the sky; they are just what Europe needs: a primordial image of innocent human behavior. They can serve as a therapy to treat the unnatural directions of the strayed creators of democracy.

The police sometimes try very brutally to move them away and prevent them drawing the attention of pedestrians, but they always find a way to start over. They persist in living in a world that is cruel toward them.

Maybe they create some disruption on the street during rush hour, but this is not the reason for why some men do not differentiate between Americans and Americans. For some police officers, every American is basically the same, at least judging by their attitude toward the Indians.

The Indians trying to conduct their "business in vain" represents the chilly change on the hot face of this increasingly Arabic city. It is the inevitable fate of many European capitals. Particularly in the case of the separation of Belgium, it could remain a natural nest for Muslims (an international city).

They will take over control very easily, because their birthrate is extremely high. Almost a third of the city's population practices Islam already. This is just a fact and not something wrong in itself. It is, perhaps, just a green version of democracy.

Brussels is a bilingual city (French and Flemish), but there is a public demand for Arabic to become an official language as well.

Flemish (a Dutch dialect) gradually disappears along with the art of their fathers. There is growing tension between them and the Arabs in one part of the country. Language is one of the main reasons for them trying to obtain their independence.

It is neither xenophobia nor a fear of Arabs, as many think, but rather a democratic version of classical Darwinism for the modern times. It is an ongoing issue for the government.

For now, the Flemish struggle for a better political position. I am no prophet, but nobody needs to be one to see the future of Brussels through the nervousness of everyday life.

Every time I see the police using force to move that peaceful company of South American Indians, I feel a panic in my heart. To see simple young girls suffer like criminals, bound by police chains, is not good entertainment.

At the same time, the extremists perform their dances, yet nobody can put them in order. I do not blame the police for doing their job, but it does pose many questions. What is our democracy in practice?

Saddam threatens again, this time with unconventional secret weapons. He points out a need to use all means necessary. According to his loudspeaker, the weapons will be deployed in the next few hours.

He commands a special task for his troops: to bring down Apaches. Because the helicopters crash down from time to time, it probably touches his imagination. Or maybe it's a desperate attempt to make his escape easier. The Apaches represent the biggest danger for him.

Some commentators take his threat very seriously. They think it could involve WMDs or a massive attack of martyrs. Others think it is just hot air, like always. In his fear, he needs something to manifest courage. Threats are his futile game.

More than 300 Iraqis were killed last night in the battle for the airport.

Another 2,500 soldiers of the Iraqi Republican Guard have surrendered to the Americans.

New suicide attacks will not help the Iraqis.

Saddam's doubles walk through Baghdad. It is like a herd of clones.

The Fedayeen express their true nature. They torture a captured female marine. However, one Iraqi shows a human face by helping the girl's friends to rescue her.

It is clear that even in the antechamber of hell, there still exists a good man. It is a good sign for those who believe the Iraqi people are different from their leaders.

The President of Egypt prophesizes that the war will create a hundred new Bin Ladens.

Iraq seems to have forgotten to use its mystery weapons. Saddam's twins and the hundred Bin Ladens could be their replacements.

Exibition or Big Apple

4/05/2003

The Iraqi press representative continues to baffle everyone. "The killers are refused, and they are permanently on fire," he said. He tries to insist the Baghdad airport is still under their control.

This improvised "gentleman" has gained a privileged status on the waves of BBC Radio London. An interview with him shows the impotent megalomania of the Iraqi government. It is an image of a disoriented society.

The Americans are nearing the center of Baghdad. It as if they walk through the streets of their homeland.

I am holding an exhibition together with around 30 other artists from Brussels. I try to be in step with the times. *"Date"* (9/11) is the title of one of my paintings.

American special units have entered the center of the Iraqi capital. The Iraqi regime dies.

My exhibition is situated in Park Elisabeth, beside the famous Basilica of the Sacred Heart of Jesus. It is a Belgian national shrine. According to its measures of grandiosity, it is the fifth greatest church in the world.

In its shadow, the paintings and sculptures give the impression of roses on the King's table. Flourished art inputs its force to spring. I cannot escape from the ghost of war.

I witness that prejudices have large eyes. If I see any Asian face, I think about SARS. If I see any Arab, I imagine the war.

Saddam's palaces are under American control. One underground shelter shows signs of WMDs.

TV channels present Baghdad like an apocalyptic vision, with Marines acting like bulldozers. Several of Saddam's monuments are demolished like the grand Buddhas of Afghanistan. It suggests that all Americans do as they like.

In spite of all this, today passes dominated by art. This does not mean that I manage to put the media out of my mind. The faces of people still speak about it.

My exhibition is entitled *The Big Apple*, a synonym for New York and a major reason for this war. Art wakes up the emotions.

One face reminded me of my recently deceased friend girl. I asked myself how many people have lost a loved one today. From time to time, I felt a pain in my soul.

At one point, a young girl cried to her grandmother, "Look at New York!" The old lady was confused.

Finally, she directed her face toward the girl's gaze. She looked at my painting, and a moment of changing colors affected her appearance. I had the impression that she became younger than anybody else around her.

I found myself in the position of a visitor, as if I saw it for the first time. God, bless all sights as a prayer from the heart for all the victims of terrorism.

I feel many Belgians love America. I believe they are the honest majority, people with a sincere heart. Anti-Americanism is a goal of the interests of evil men.

For a long time, I dream about my journey to follow the steps of my grandfathers. I want to touch the Big Apple with my own fingers.

Prediction

4/06/2003

The fear caused by SARS spreads its mystery.

One Belgian couple refused to marry in the town hall because a young Chinese couple, recently arrived from China, was married in the building some days before.

The British perform something resembling a dance around Basra. They step up and forward. They take two steps back then make three aggressive ones, and so on. They don't need to point out that they are not in a hurry.

It seems the Americans will capture Baghdad easier than the other cities.

For an instant, I have the impression that the European demonstrations have faded like a lilting flower. There is a silence like you find during a penalty in a soccer match. In no time, they will be shouting again. However, I feel their logic is different than at a stadium. Some people always make a lot of noise without reason.

The loudspeakers of the Jihad arise like apocalyptic messengers worldwide. In the media, the jihadists are at home.

However, Christ will arrive suddenly, like a thief in the night, to judge the world. It will be like the time of Noah. I see some people and their ideologies as a flood.

He will come after the great disturbance of everything. The Bible says that people will be occupied with everyday life during that time. It is proof that many will survive our stupidities. Apocalypse is not as dark as our imaginations.

One German historian predicts that America cannot capture the Iraqi capital, because every large city is capable of resisting. He compares it with Stalingrad.

Then, he speaks about the 30,000 civilians who perished during the bombing of Hamburg. He thinks the US cannot put such a cross on its back again.

From that point of view, people are more faithful to their leaders during wartime.

While many talk of stories and predictions, the Marines continue to fight. About 2,000 Iraqi soldiers have died so far.

Richard Pearle (of the Pentagon) predicted that the war would end in only six weeks.

I try to take some free time and fight against the media terror.

I describe spring in Brussels through the window of my room. It's a sunny day, and a walnut tree manifests its first buds. Some plants are already enjoying their green dresses.

Some birds sing better than I could ever imagine. Some pigeons fall in love. I wash my eyes with this message. I enjoy my yearnings.

The fighting continues around Baghdad airport, but the Americans are there and already using it.

Some Iraqis deny that any Iraqi will welcome the Americans as friends. They see that expectation as an illusion. Although they do not love Saddam, they like him more than they do cowboys.

On the way from Baghdad to Syria, a Russian diplomatic convoy was caught in the crossfire. Some people are wounded.

I ask myself why the Russians did not leave before. Why do they choose to go now? Is Saddam with them? Are the WMDs with them? How much money are they carrying? Is it a diplomatic mission or a criminal endeavor?

A helicopter crashed down again. It was the last flight for three marines.

The Muslims continue to urge their brothers and sisters to respond to their message of Jihad. They cannot accept that America is helping Arabs to be free.

Today is Sunday, and I listen to some classical music in my favorite church. I try to pray to the rhythm of Bach's symphonies. I recollect the prayer from the beginning of my diary.

I remember Bush's words when he said he prays for peace. He is the first Christian political leader to say this in the 21st century. I do not remember any other political leaders saying it. Western civilization does not like such men. Our time has strayed in its liberal atheism, and the occult agnostic indifference silently reforms all religions.

Many Europeans, in their atheism, are incapable of understanding believers. The law becomes too aggressive against Christians. There is no peace for the future of Europe without the conversion of all Europeans. It travels into its abyss.

An American fighter killed some Americans. They were soldiers who fought with the Kurds in the north of Iraq.

Baghdad is out of Saddam's control; his army acts without any serious strategy.

A key point to the southeast of the city is a bridge over the Tigris.

The Pope asks for the end of the war as soon as possible. The Americans are obliging.

About 2,600 people in 30 countries are affected by SARS.

China hides the truth about the virus. I am not surprised.

The national emblem of that Asian titan is a dragon. It is easy to recognize it as the famous apocalyptic red serpent. I say that because of its communist nature. I did not say that its clay (china) will bear the serpent, nor do I say the Chinese are devils. There are too many demons already.

Powell has apologized to Russia for the convoy attack.

There is speculation that some animals can spread the SARS virus. Evidently, it is time to destroy animals as well as people.

The whole world speaks about the war and SARS like pupils speak about their homework. Some think that SARS is a consequence of the American strategy to divert attention from the war.

One camp of jihadists is bombed. There are many martyrs out there. Martyr is a misused word by many, but especially by the media.

This day is also marked with painful images of innocent victims. One so-called smart bomb is confused and forgets that the Hotel Palestine is a key point for many journalists. Many are very angry at America. I hate smart bombs, because some can be stupid.

To finish this day, I put my prediction onto paper: One day, the majority of Muslims could be acting like American bombs, not just the extremists as has happened so far.

The Jihad takes wing.

Russian Convoy

4/07/2003

Today is International Health Day, so it seems that SARS dominates over the war.

The Americans control all the roads into Baghdad. The city is now completely besieged.

In the skies above Iraq, there are 1,000 fighter jets every day.

The Iraqi press representative radiates the culmination of hypocrisy. "God will deliver the victory to God's people," he said. This is just what many Americans want.

He talks like he did at the beginning of the war. I'm not always sure he knows what he is speaking about. However, this time he spoke the truth despite himself, and for the first time, many believe him. He did not change, but he really does not know what is happening there.

I conclude that a man sometimes needs to be a very delicate observer to comprehend the difference between things that appear the same at first sight. This time, our beliefs are a very important difference.

If I touch one of my hands, I always feel that the hand I touched is weaker than the one I used. At that moment, it is not important which hand is left or right. It proves that attack is the best defense.

Some people know that better than others. One Russian journalist blames the Americans for the crossfire incident. He believes it was intentional. Evidently, he is better informed than others.

It restarts an old game. With a smell from the time of the Cold War, I write these words.

I use my experience to destroy the kingdom of lies. I know truth is always power.

One time, a German woman told a man that he was an idiot because he insisted on protecting his human rights in spite of her. "Maybe I am," he answered, "but only at first sight."

Today, I see the Russian convoy as a parade of idiots, and I would prefer not to believe that it is not just at first sight. I say that respecting their great writer Dostoyevsky. He told that to them and other idiots as well.

Many make decisions based on initial appearance, so many are idiots at the start and the end, in spite of them and in spite of us.

However, many are wrongly judged at first sight, and this is only so at that moment. If the world would lose these idiots, who are not idiots, it would also lose its chance to survive. Therefore, I feel the suffering of many because they are so many idiots.

Saddam's residences are without Saddam to show his face in now.

Panic rules the Iraqis all over the country.

Apocalyptic images dominate the media. Thousands of wounded civilians, hundreds killed, buildings on fire or in ruins, and so on.

It is the price of freedom, despite the idiots.

"There are no Americans in Baghdad," said the already famous Iraqi press representative.

Iraqi refugees trained in Europe start to fight for the freedom of their country. They have dreamed for a long time.

I try to forget the Russian convoy.

Amnesty International

4/08/2003

It is the hunt for Saddam. There is fighting in the center of Baghdad as American tanks cross over the Tigris.

The battle starts for the underground city. The 10,000 meters of labyrinth-like corridors below the surface could be Saddam's last residence.

The doors of these hell-rooms are made strong enough to withstand even a nuclear attack. Evidently, Saddam is ready to refuse even atomic gifts!

The Americans deny again that they intentionally targeted the troubled Russian convoy. The Russian ambassador was injured. In fact, all of them were hurt.

The new 66th US Secretary of State, Condoleezza Rice, visited Moscow. Sometimes, nobody can explain anything to some people.

Many Russians think that American money is so powerful that nobody is capable of withstanding the force of the US. They are afraid that America could attack them one day like they have Iraq.

Bush and Blair have organized a summit in Northern Ireland. People are not afraid of them there like they are in Russia. It is their fourth time together this year. Can anybody believe that it is not because of the almost-defeated Iraq?

A new story about the liquidation of Saddam amuses everybody again.

The British dance around Basra is finally finished. It is a free city now, although many feel like they are in a British detention center.

Over Baghdad, the smell of smoke and liberty is mixed with fears of an apocalyptic time.

The Amnesty International of Belgium informs its members about its annual convention. There will be an opportunity to speak about the issues of our time. I would like to speak about the moral harassment of the media.

Maybe I have it wrong, and they are just serving the psychology of the masses. Some people think that organized disorders move the world.

A lost sense asks for the nature of understanding the relationships among people. The current time systematically loses the primordial base of love.

I am afraid of the distorted contemporary virtues, because humanity lacks the courage to change them. Is this a main reason for the Second Coming of Jesus Christ? Evidently, his time comes!

Some European countries are the best example of this progression of moral chaos. They even allow same-sex couples to adopt children, although the most of them do not want it. I am no lawbreaker, but I think that since the time of Babylon, no civilization has strayed so deep into the darkness of nothingness.

The birth rate of native Belgians is very low, like it is among all European nations. Maybe some know that life exists in the kingdom of death and follow it.

European roots go to the other side!

Maybe I exaggerate, and the future belongs to the genetic engineering of children from test tubes or adopting Chinese children or those of our brothers and sisters from different religious roots.

Therefore, the modern age progresses, and some might see it just as an advanced measure to stabilize the birthrate. I am sorry that I am so out of date. However, I still think that I have the right to form my own opinions!

I do not understand the new European wave of anti-Semitism and anti-Americanism. It shows blind solidarity with the terrorists. It is a clear image of many people and many governments. Someone could perceive it imprinted in the European manifestations and demonstrations.

Islam has developed its roots, and thus the jihadists have conquered many Christian lands. The main reason for their success was their sword. It would be a grim vision of the time to come if their weapons dominated over America.

Egypt was once a Christian land in the seventh century. Today it is a source of terrorism. I say all that I do because I feel the EU follows the fate of the Mason's pyramids.

The hunt for Saddam becomes very interesting.

As I mentioned earlier, his idol is the former Yugoslavian dictator Tito. If you understand Tito's history, it is easier to follow Saddam's path. Therefore, his only shelter will be found in Russia or in some cave somewhere.

Many citizens of Basra welcome the British as friends.

I do not know anybody who likes to help refugees, but Amnesty International demands better protection of the Iraqi refugees. Its efforts often seem like dewdrops confronted by the rays of sun. However, it is true that winds sometimes move the clouds in a better direction.

Britain tests a new bomb. It detonates without the sound of explosion. Maybe, it does not wish to disturb its enemy (or even Amnesty International)!

Lasso Finish

4/09/2003

The final moments of the Iraqi regime are here without any doubt. In spite of the many superstitious comments, nobody can change the future. It's game over.

The Chinese lies make SARS a more mysterious ailment than it really is. The scientists advise many measures for protection. I am afraid it will soon be forbidden to look at oneself in the mirror.

It is a time of TV drama. A monument of Saddam, somewhere in Baghdad, suffers a decisive attack from his revolting slaves. It is a comedy and a tragedy.

It is all shown live. This is the very art of the fixed camera.

An American soldier on top of a tank reminds me of Moses during the time of Pesach.

Euphoria makes courageous people from the citizens. Some exercise the force of superheroes.

It is a case of hammer and hammer. Many try to hammer their anger into Saddam's biography. There are Iraqis and Americans. It seems that Saddam's monument resists them.

They write a New Time. It is history.

It is a moment for vengeance. There is hate in the heart of the slaves, and it is time to quench their thirsts.

The commentators on the Arab networks cannot hide their tears.

Dick Cheney (vice-president of the US) has declared, "Iraq is free."

The masses are crazy. People are in a state of delirium. Saddam pictures burn like witches on the stake. It points out American flags all over the country.

There is euphoria, and all the good and bad that go together, we can see there.

For a moment, I feel the spirit of the media as a vibration of goodwill.

A strange silence takes power over the battlefield. Are the pockets of resistance just a sign of the end?

It smells like peace, even as tanks pass through Baghdad. For a moment, even lies are out of any opposition.

New comments by the anti-American media give the impression of birds caught in an oil spill. Some try to be funny, but they are merely naive anti-Americans. Humor cannot wash their oil-drenched heads.

Around Saddam's monument, the American soldiers take a leading role. It seems like they're improvising the scene of a movie like a Hollywood studio.

The face of the statue is covered by the American flag. The Iraqi banner serves as a tie. Iraqis move like entranced dancers around the totemic symbol of their clown king.

It is a party, with people enjoying their freedom more than on some American streets.

A tank pulls on Saddam's statue using an iron chain lassoed around its colossal neck. The Marines help the citizens who desperately try to bring down their titan.

It is easy to imagine an iron cowboy in the saddle of an iron horse. However, it is without any doubt a cowboy rite. They do not like totems.

The monument is uprooted. For an instant, it hangs over its pedestal like the Antichrist on an inverted cross.

It is a time of upside-down art. However, this act is a greater artistic expression than the original creation of that concrete monster.

Will the Iraqis know how to keep their freedom?

For a moment, some become converted pro-Americans. Together with his followers, they shout, "Hero!" to Bush. However, many need more time to admit their mistakes. Many will stay blind forever in spite of all this because it is their nature.

I remember the comments of Nelson Mandela and some other improvised saints in the days before the war. For an instant, they all lost their charisma together with the shameful face of the media. They need to take a deep breath before they open their mouths again.

The Mujahedin also lack the courage to say God is still on their side. He left them, or they have mistakenly thought that God holds out human flags.

It seems that it all happened like a desert slalom through Iraq. I am not sure that anybody could follow it, not even Janica Kostelic (a Croatian skiing phenomenon).

The lost media try to retain their imagined dignity. They say that Saddam's regime did not collapse because of American force but rather because of the will of the Iraqi people.

I turn off the TV. I try to be trendy, so I go to the city to buy some white color for my new paintings.

One woman weeps at the exit of a metro station. I can see her Maghrebian face without a scarf.

I look at two taxi drivers, Arabs, in the center of Brussels near to the Church of Saint Nicola. One gives the impression of a very important messenger with breaking news, while the other is ready to wash his car with his tears.

Why some people cry this afternoon is not a question for me. Everybody has their own reasons, and I understand sometimes.

It was a painful lasso finish.

Liberty

4/10/2003

Freedom is like love. It has a need to be realized by everybody. It is the turn of the Iraqis.

Some Muslims think that God left Saddam because he was not a good Muslim.

The snow does not like Brussels. It rarely visits the capital of Europe and the headquarters of NATO, but it is snowing now. It is always a feast for my heart. I enjoy whiteness.

This time I feel the suffering of spring. Nature has been wounded in its infancy, but I know it will flourish again soon. I know Iraq will also be renewed one day.

It seems that the whole world hurries to take part in rebuilding it. Again, the loudest countries are those who opposed the war. They always know their interests. I think many are lost in time and space because of the power of their mirror.

It is sunny again.

Greed is a more dangerous disease than SARS. Some believe that SARS could take more victims than all the storms over Iraq. It is really an irony that the innocent Chinese spread fear like terrorists.

This spring changes things very fast. Already everybody knows something about SARS, so I therefore believe only the Chinese seem so dangerous.

I am not afraid of the Apocalypse, because I see there is more light than darkness. I believe in the triumph of Mercy of God, and I trust in Jesus!

Three weeks already, and the revolting imaginations of some anti-American journalists try to ridicule the facts. Today is the first day that I cannot read about Bush being a killer, butcher, or whatever. It is a new face from the newspapers. Many are like the Belgian French-language daily *Le Soir* when they say, *"Very good America."*

However, Le Monde is one of the most disappointed papers. I compare it to the Arab media, although I cannot read Arabic.

Many journalists have lost their moral code. This is a consequence of general disorder. In a time of political insecurity, such people are not capable of stepping forward, because they cannot see the light we need to follow.

Bush and Blair spread the message to the Iraqis in the Arabic language.

Their reply is a new suicide attack.

Some 105 American soldiers have died so far. This number reminds me of the Bible Code.

Humor has changed its side. Some Americans claim that Saddam has escaped to France.

There is chaos on the streets of Baghdad with looting and raping. For now, the Marines are unable to control the rampaging citizens.

In spite of all this, humanitarian questions dominate the media. I think it is time to finish my diary.

Although some call SARS the travel killer, I have decided to travel regardless. I have changed my destination, however. I would like to visit Salt Lake City. I see one of the most moral parts of our civilization there, a little like Croatia in Europe.

However, I primarily want to go there to light a candle for my grandfather, a hero of America and an honored citizen of the state of Utah.

The Tigris flows.
The Euphrates flows.

I try to forget that paradise.
Let the bird of Eden flutter up its wings...

Hunt for Saddam

4/11/2003

The Kingdom of Belgium prepares for the wedding of its young prince and his English-born princess.

President George W. Bush declares, "I do not know where Saddam is, but I know he has no control over Iraq."

It was 22 days on the journey to Baghdad.

For some, a question still occupies them: Was Iraq the best choice? Others wonder whether it needs to be the only target.

I think most of us know the answers to both questions!

For some other people, these will forever be unsolved questions, because they do not comprehend what the Jihad really means.

I continue to pray to Saint Michael.

THE END

P.S.
I wrote down the facts and my opinions about them. I do not judge anybody, nor do I want anybody to judge others because of my words...

Author
Ivan Herceg writes in Croatian, French, and English. He is the author of various books.

-

www.ingramcontent.com/pod-product-compliance
Lightning Source LLC
Chambersburg PA
CBHW070429290526
45791CB00005B/1900